LEAN
PRODUCTION
SIMPLIFIED

A Plain-Language Guide to the World's Most
Powerful Production System

THIRD EDITION

LEAN

PRODUCTION

SIMPLIFIED

A Plain-Language Guide to the World's Most Powerful Production System

THIRD EDITION

PASCAL DENNIS

FOREWORD BY JOHN SHOOK

CRC Press
Taylor & Francis Group
Boca Raton London New York

CRC Press is an imprint of the
Taylor & Francis Group, an **informa** business

A PRODUCTIVITY PRESS BOOK

CRC Press
Taylor & Francis Group
6000 Broken Sound Parkway NW, Suite 300
Boca Raton, FL 33487-2742

© 2015 by Pascal Dennis
CRC Press is an imprint of Taylor & Francis Group, an Informa business

No claim to original U.S. Government works

Printed on acid-free paper
Version Date: 20160115

International Standard Book Number-13: 978-1-4987-0887-6 (Paperback)

Visit the Taylor & Francis Web site at
http://www.taylorandfrancis.com

and the CRC Press Web site at
http://www.crcpress.com

In memory of Roger Komer (1946–2006)
We miss you, amigo

Contents

Foreword xv

Preface xvii

About the Author xxiii

Introduction xxv

1 The Birth of Lean 1

Craft Production 1

Mass Production 2

Ford System 3

Other Developments 5

Growing Dysfunction 6

    Worker Alienation 6

    Quality 7

    Machinery 7

    Engineering 7

Birth of Lean Production 8

    Historic Bargain 9

    A Novel Concept 12

    A Virtue of Necessity 12

Completing the Lean Revolution at Toyota 13

Summary 14

Reference 15

Endnotes 15

Study Questions 17

2 Lean Production System **19**

Why Lean Production? 19

New Economics 19

Systems and Systems Thinking 21

The "Thinking Way" 23

Basic Image of Lean Production 24

Customer Focus 28

Muda 29

Motion 30

Delay 31

Conveyance 32

Correction 32

Overprocessing 32

Inventory 32

Overproduction 33

Knowledge 33

A Word of Caution 34

Mura 35

Muri 36

Summary 36

Endnotes 36

Study Questions 38

3 Stability **39**

Lean System Standards 39

Visual Management 42

5S System 44

S1—Sort 45

Just-in-Case Management 45

Red Tagging 45

S2—Set in Order 47

Rationalize Locations 47

Organize and Apply Colors 48

S3—Shine (and Inspect) 49

S4—Standardize 49

Standards for S1 to S3 51

S5—Sustain 51

5S Promotion and Communication 52

5S Training 52

Total Productive Maintenance 53
  Key Measures 54
  Six Big Losses...55
    Downtime...55
    Speed or Hidden Losses 55
    Defects..55
  The Machine Loss Pyramid 57
  Small-Group Activity 59
Summary 59
Endnotes..61
Study Questions 63

4 Standardized Work 65
Methods Engineering versus Lean Thinking 65
What Do We Have to Manage?..66
  Maximize Utilization of Machines or People?....................................67
  Labor Density 68
Why Standardized Work?..68
  Prerequisites for Standardized Work 69
Elements of Standardized Work 71
  Takt Time 71
  Takt Time and Cycle Time...71
  Work Sequence 72
  In-Process Stock 72
Charts Used to Define Standardized Work 73
  Production Capacity Chart..73
  Standardized Work Combination Table..74
  Standardized Work Analysis Chart 75
  Job Element Sheets..76
  Time Measurement..76
Manpower Reduction...78
Overall Efficiency versus Individual Efficiency....................................80
Standardized Work and Kaizen..82
  Guidelines for Economy of Motion 82
  Guidelines for Layout and Equipment...82
  Guidelines for Tools and Jigs..83
Common Layouts 83
  Islands..84
  Connected Islands..84

Connected Islands with Full-Work Control 84

Cells 84

Summary 84

Endnotes..86

Study Questions 88

5 Just-in-Time Production 89

Why JIT?..89

Basic Principles of JIT..92

Continuous Flow 92

Pull...93

The JIT System 96

Kanban...96

Kanban Metaphors...99

Pacemaker Process..100

The Store 101

Six Kanban Rules 102

Rule 1: Never Ship Defective Items 102

Rule 2: The Customer Withdraws Only What Is Needed.............102

Rule 3: Produce Only the Quantity Withdrawn by the Customer 103

Rule 4: Level Production 103

Rule 5: Use Kanban to Fine-Tune Production................................104

Rule 6: Stabilize and Strengthen the Process 104

Expanded Role of Conveyance..105

How Frequently Should We Provide Production Orders?...................106

Quick Adjustment to Demand Changes or Other Sources of

Instability..106

Better Sense of Takt Time 106

Fewer Peaks and Valleys...107

Abnormality Control 107

Two Kinds of Conveyance..107

Production Leveling 108

Responding to Changes in Customer Demand...................................110

Heijunka Box...111

Three Types of Pull Systems 112

Type A Pull System 112

Type B Pull System 112

Type C Pull System 113

Value Stream Mapping 114

Summary 119
Endnotes... 119
Study Questions 121

6 Jidoka...**123**
Development of the Jidoka Concept 123
Why Jidoka?... 124
  How to Improve Human Reliability 127
Poka-Yoke 127
  Common Errors... 127
Inspection Systems and Zone Control 128
  Judgment Inspections—Discovering Defects................... 128
  Informative Inspections—Reducing Defects 129
  Source Inspections—Preventing Defects 129
    Vertical Source Inspections.. 129
    Horizontal Source Inspections..................................... 129
Using Poka-Yokes 131
  Two Types of Action 131
    Shutdown.. 131
    Warning 132
  Three Paths to Poka-Yoke.. 132
    Work Piece Deviations 132
    Work Method Deviations 133
    Deviations from Fixed Values...................................... 133
  Poka-Yoke Detection Methods... 134
    Contact Sensors 134
    Noncontact Methods 134
Implementing Jidoka.. 137
  Annual Jidoka Strategy and Goals................................... 138
  Future Directions 138
Summary 139
Endnotes... 140
Study Questions 141

7 Involvement **143**
Why Involvement?... 143
Terrible Waste of Humanity.. 145
Activities Supporting Involvement....................................... 146
  Goal of Involvement 146

Kaizen Circle Activity...148

    Structure of KCA 148

    KCA Training..148

    KCA Administration 149

    KCA Promotion 150

    Role of the Manager...151

Practical Kaizen Training...152

    Key Factors for PKT Success..153

        Communication 153

        Grasping the Situation...153

        Problem Solving 154

        Role of the Supervisor...154

Suggestion Programs...154

    Hassle-Free Process and Clear Rules.......................................155

    Tangible Suggestions..155

    Intangible Suggestions 156

    Quick Decision-Making and Feedback 156

    Fairness..156

    Promotion...156

    Extrinsic and Intrinsic Motivation...157

    How to Motivate Suggestions 157

    Quantity First—Then Quality 158

    Annual Culture Hoshin 158

  Summary 159

  Endnotes..159

  Study Questions 160

8 Hoshin Planning.. 161

What Is Planning?..162

Why Plan?...163

Problems with Planning...163

    How Do We Create Flow?..164

Hoshin Planning 165

    Focus of Hoshin Planning 165

    Alignment and Flexibility..166

        Hoshin Planning and MBO...168

Hoshin Planning System..169

    PDCA 169

    Check Outcomes and Process 170

Strengthen People 170

Nemawashi 171

Catchball 172

The Control Department Concept 174

A3 Thinking 176

History of Report Writing 177

Common Report-Writing Problems 177

The Four Phases of Hoshin Planning 180

Hoshin Generation 180

Hoshin Deployment 182

Output of Hoshin Deployment 182

Hoshin Implementation 187

Hoshin Evaluation 187

Book of Knowledge 187

Summary 188

Endnotes 188

Study Questions 190

9 The Culture of Lean Production 191

What Is Lean Culture? 192

PDCA 192

Grasping the Situation (GTS) 194

Plan 194

Do 195

Check 195

Act 196

Reflection—Breakfast of Champions 196

Warm Heart Principle 197

Standardization 197

Standards and Abnormality Control 199

Visual Management 200

Management as Theater 200

Teamwork 200

Paradox 202

Intensity 202

Lean Production as a Path 203

How Does Lean Culture Feel? 203

Summary 204

Final Comments 204
Endnotes...205
Study Questions 206

Glossary..**207**

Bibliography...**211**

Index **215**

Foreword

"Not another 'Introduction to Lean' book" was my immediate reaction upon hearing from Pascal his plans for this Lean production overview. Surely, I thought, we have plenty of books that cover the topic, maybe too many. After all, the basics, merits, and various aspects of the system have been chronicled in countless books, journal articles, research reports, seminars, and lectures, especially since James Womack, Dan Jones, and their researcher John Krafcik coined the term "Lean production" in 1989. Then Pascal gave me the chance to read his manuscript. And I was convinced. There is a need for a book exactly like this, and Pascal has the experience, knowledge, and passion to write it.

Pascal Dennis is one of many Westerners who, during the past 20 years, have gained firsthand experience with "Lean production" or the Toyota Production System (TPS). At Toyota Motor Manufacturing Canada, one of Toyota's early and successful efforts to transplant TPS outside the confines of Toyota City in Japan, Pascal received personalized mentoring from his trainer from Toyota City about each of the processes, systems, and philosophies explained in this book. Pascal allows us to share in his discoveries while taking us through the basics of the system in a commonsense, step-by-step fashion. Much of the contents of this primer could be taken verbatim from Toyota training manuals, whereas others reflect Pascal's own, personal learning. That is as it should be. As each of us encounters this body of knowledge and experience, we borrow from the learnings of those who have preceded us and we add in our own unique experiences and perspectives.

I suggest that, as you read this book, you consider yourself a fellow sojourner with Pascal along a path of Lean discovery. This book may answer some questions for you, but those questions are only the beginning, really. As one of my own senseis taught me along the way, "Some of us may become teachers (and authors), but we are all learners, first and last." This book is a great way to begin learning.

It is well known that TPS developer Taiichi Ohno was highly skeptical of learning that was not based on the plant floor. In fact, the early chroniclers of TPS within Toyota were forced to sequester themselves away in hidden rooms to work on their writings back in the early 1970s for fear of being admonished by Ohno: "If you have so much time on your hands, get out on the plant floor!" But, eventually even he wrote books (and you may want to choose his own *Toyota Production System* as your next reading after finishing this book!). There are many facets to Lean production and many paths to learning. Reading can be one of them. But let's also remind ourselves of Ohno's advice: "The real learning will take place where the action is, so get out there and try, fail, and try again!"

John Shook
Senior Advisor, Lean Enterprise Institute
President, TWI Network, Inc.
Ann Arbor, Michigan

Preface

Less is more.

Robert Browning

I began my journey of discovery as a graduate student in 1981 when I saw a CBS documentary entitled *If Japan Can, Why Can't We?* featuring an old dude named W. Edwards Deming. The sight of Deming excoriating top executives like an *Old Testament* prophet made a deep impression on me. I began my management career seeking out everything I could find by Deming and Joseph Juran.

I was already familiar with Japanese culture through my study of aikido. I had spent many hours in the Toronto Aikikai dojo[1] practicing the powerful circular movements. I couldn't have imagined that my aikido training would prove useful on the Toyota shop floor.

In 1986 I read *The Reckoning*,[2] David Halberstam's classic account of North American industry in crisis. Halberstam's Toyota seemed a shining city on the hill, driven by humane values, and prospering even in the worst of times. In 1992 Womack et al. published *The Machine That Changed the World*[3] and proved what everyone suspected: something remarkable was happening there.

Fortunately for me, Toyota Motor Manufacturing Canada was just down Highway 401. I applied for a job and was accepted, and my apprenticeship began in earnest. I felt I was a student in a dojo once again, though it took me years to unlearn all the bad habits I had accumulated. Gradually, I began to see and think clearly.

The journey has transformed me. The Toyota Production System, or Lean production, is a *do,* or path, that I will walk the rest of my life. I believe, with Jim Womack and Dan Jones, that in the twenty-first century, Lean thinking will dramatically boost productivity, while sharply reducing errors, accidents, space requirements, time-to-market, and costs in general. The world will indeed be a better place.

Objectives

Few of my readers will have had the opportunity to see Toyota up close. My objective is to provide a clear and simple guide to Lean production: its components, how they fit together, and the spirit that animates them. To the greatest extent possible, I wish to make explicit what is implicit in the Toyota system. I can hope only for partial success. Some things can be learned only on the shop floor. Nonetheless, I perceive a strong need for this book.

Lean production is first and foremost a system, that is, an integrated series of parts with a clearly defined goal. One of the problems with Lean implementation has been the tendency to cherry-pick activities, rather than grasping the system as a whole.

We are hindered by our enchantment with fragmentation. I am reminded of the Indian fable about the blind men trying to describe the elephant. "The elephant is long and sharp, like a sword," says the man holding the elephant's tusk. "No, he is wide and flat as a table top," says the man feeling the elephant's belly. "No, he is wide and floppy like a lettuce leaf," says the man feeling the beast's ear.

Moreover, few appreciate the spirit that animates the Toyota system. Its best expression is the personal motto of an esteemed sensei[4]: open mind, teamwork, challenge. The Lean shop floor is a daunting, exhilarating place.

This indomitable and humane spirit is the "wind that fills the sails." The most adroitly designed system is lifeless without it, akin to a beautiful sailboat without the life-giving breeze.

Robert Browning could not have imagined that his famous aphorism would one day find expression in a book on manufacturing. But then, the word *poetry* is derived from the Greek word *poesis*, "to make things." And Lean production is a seamless tapestry of art and science.

Intended Audience

This book is written for
- Managers responsible for production, quality, cost, or safety
- Executives and senior managers with a strategic interest in Lean production

- Quality, maintenance, and human resources professionals
- Engineers and scientists
- Safety and environment professionals
- Students engaged in management studies
- Anybody interested in management excellence

Structure of the Book

Chapter 1 describes the craft and mass production systems that preceded Lean production. The contributions of Frederick Winslow Taylor and Henry Ford and the strengths and weaknesses of mass production are discussed. The business environment that Toyota faced in 1950 was the catalyst for the Toyota Production System, the world's foremost example of Lean production. Lean production is vital today because we face precisely the same challenges that Toyota faced in 1950.

Chapter 2 discusses the Lean production system. I introduce the House of Lean Production, around which the book is organized. The eight kinds of *muda* (waste) are illustrated. The effects of overproduction, the most serious form of waste, are highlighted. The related concepts of *mura* (unevenness) and *muri* (strain) are also illustrated. A central goal of Lean production is to improve profitability by reducing waste.

Chapter 3 deals with stability, the foundation of the Lean system. Standards in the Lean system are contrasted with conventional standards. The concept of visual management is introduced. 5S, a system of workplace organization and standardization, is described. Total productive maintenance (TPM) is the key to machine stability.

Chapter 4 deals with standardized work. Lean production views standardized work differently than does industrial engineering. The elements of standardized work are illustrated. The purpose of standardized work is kaizen.[5]

Chapter 5 deals with just-in-time delivery of parts and products, the key to reducing the mudas of overproduction, inventory, and defects. The concepts of continuous flow and pull are discussed. The kanban system is described in detail including different kinds of kanban and the six kanban rules. The three kinds of pull systems are described. Production leveling is a prerequisite for flow and pull. Value stream mapping is demonstrated using a case study.

Chapter 6 addresses the jidoka principle. Jidoka entails developing processes that are capable and do not pass defects to the next process. The poka-yoke[6] principle, a paradigm shift beyond statistical process control, is outlined. The role of jidoka in supporting stability and continuous flow is explained. The relationship between jidoka, visual management, and involvement is elucidated.

Chapter 7 deals with involvement, the heart of the Lean system. Kaizen circle activity, practical kaizen training, and suggestion systems are described in detail. The role of the manager and supervisor in supporting and sustaining involvement is highlighted.

Chapter 8 describes hoshin planning, the nervous system of Lean production. Hoshin planning seeks to overcome the management disconnects that lead to the muda of knowledge. The hoshin planning system comprises plan–do–check–act (PDCA), catchball, nemawashi, the control department concept, and A3 thinking, each of which is discussed in this chapter. Hoshin planning is described as a pull system; that is, our vision pulls us into the future.

Chapter 9 deals with the culture of Lean production. Its cornerstones are PDCA, standardization, visual management, teamwork, paradox, and intensity. Lean production is a *do*, or path, that must be approached with a spirit of humility and lifelong learning.

A Note on Terminology

The glossary is a listing of Lean terms and concepts. I have tried to use English terms where possible. Japanese terms are used where they are well known or convey an added level of meaning.

Acknowledgments

I would like to thank the editorial staff at Productivity Press for their help and support, and in particular, Michael Sinocchi, senior editor. I am indebted to my friend and colleague, Erik Hager, for many fruitful discussions on the ideas outlined herein. Indeed, many are his own. Thanks also to John Shook for his thoughtful feedback.

Special thanks to my senseis—Hiroyuki Watanabe, Tak Sakaue, Shin Furukawa, Daryl Wilson, and John Shook—with whom it has been my privilege to work. I hope they will overlook any shortcomings in this book.

Finally, I would like to thank Toyota Motor Corporation, which continues to be a beacon to organizations around the world, and whose remarkable generosity and openness are helping to make a better world.

Long may you run.

Endnotes

1. Training hall.
2. David Halberstram, *The Reckoning* (New York: Bantam Books, 1984).
3. James Womack, Daniel Jones, and Daniel Roos, *The Machine That Changed the World* (New York: Simon & Schuster, 1990).
4. *Sensei* means one who has gone before.
5. *Kaizen* means continuous incremental improvement.
6. A *poka-yoke* is a device that prevents a defect from progressing to the next process.

About the Author

Pascal Dennis, P.Eng., M.Eng., is a professional engineer, author, and president of Lean Pathways, an international consultancy. Pascal developed his skills on the Toyota shop floor in North America and Japan and by working with major international companies.

The winner of four Shingo Prizes for Excellence, Pascal has supported breakthrough improvement in healthcare, software development, financial services, construction, and the consumer goods and process industries. The focus of his practice is strategic planning and execution, executive coaching, and growing intellectual capital. For more information please visit www.leansystems.org or Pascal's Amazon page: www.amazon.com/Pascal-Dennis/e/B001JS3XTW.

About the Author

Introduction

The more I know, the more I realize I don't know.

Socrates

I wrote the first edition of *Lean Production Simplified* hoping to share what I'd learned at Toyota. It had been my blind luck to work with patient *senseis*.[1] I felt that if I could explain things simply, then perhaps I had gained a certain level of understanding. For the past 16 years, I have been the sensei, helping companies apply the Toyota system or "Lean." My practice has taken me far from the Toyota shop floor into hospitals, power plants, container terminals, and research laboratories. I'm certain that I *learn* as much as I *teach*. And the more I learn, the more I think of Socrates.

We need to learn the Toyota system, and not just in manufacturing. The stakes are higher than ever. Hospitals, banks, universities, software developers, government agencies, and other service providers are also in trouble. Customers will no longer accept substandard safety, quality, delivery, or cost performance. Jobs that seemed secure a few years ago are withering like autumn leaves.

My study of aikido had prepared me for the Toyota "way." I understood that it was a *do*,[2] or path, and that the Toyota shop floor was a *dojo*,[3] a place where you practiced a profound art, working on your technique, and on yourself. Indeed, before stepping on to the shop floor, I felt like bowing, a sign of respect for my team, organization, and the art of management.

I still feel that way. Enjoy the journey.

Endnotes

1. *Sensei* means "one who has gone before."

2. *Do* means "way" or "path." A set of methods or techniques becomes a do when it connects to one's whole being.
3. *Dojo* means "training hall."

Chapter 1

The Birth of Lean

There are some possibilities to improve the production system...

Eiji Toyoda at Ford Rouge plant, circa 1950

New ideas are a response to concrete problems. To understand Lean production we need to understand the mass production system that it is supplanting.[1] Let us take a brief historical tour.[2-5]

Craft Production

If you wanted to buy a car in 1900, for example, you would have visited one of the craft producers in your area. The shop owner, usually an entrepreneur who did a range of manufacturing and repair work, would take your specifications. Several months later you would get your car. You would roadtest it, accompanied by a mechanic, who would modify it to your liking. The car would be one of a kind, and the cost would be high. But you would have the satisfaction of dealing directly with the manufacturer and his team.

Craft production had the following characteristics:

- A workforce comprising quasi-independent tradesmen skilled at design, machining, and fitting.
  - Decentralized organization. Small machine shops provided most parts. The owner/entrepreneur coordinated the process in direct contact with contractors, workers, and customers.

- General-purpose machines. These were used for cutting, drilling, and grinding of parts.
■ Low production volumes and high prices.

Craft production continues to survive in tiny niches, usually for luxury products. For example, companies including Lamborghini, Ferrari, and Aston Martin continue to produce small volumes of very expensive automobiles for buyers seeking prestige and the opportunity to deal directly with the factory.

Nostalgists look on craft production as a golden era when craftsmanship counted and companies gave personal attention to each customer. This is true, but there were major disadvantages:

■ Only the rich could afford the product.
■ Quality was unpredictable; each product was essentially a prototype.
■ Improvement activities were not widely shared. In fact, some trade organizations saw improvement as a threat.
■ Henry Ford and Fred Winslow Taylor sought to overcome these problems.

Mass Production

Fred Winslow Taylor, a foundry manager from Philadelphia, laid the foundation for mass production.[6] He was the first to systematically apply scientific principles to manufacturing. His landmark text, *Scientific Management*,[7] remains a classic. The craft system was largely empirical, depending on the experience of the tradesman.[8] Taylor sought to identify the "best way" to do the job based on scientific principles. In doing so, he invented industrial engineering.

Taylor's system was based on separating planning from production. Industrial engineers, through new techniques such as time and motion studies, would determine the "best way" to do the job, leaving the workforce to do the short cycle, repetitive tasks. The basic premise of the Taylor system was that the workforce lacked the literacy needed to plan the work. Taylor's premise may have been valid at the turn of the last century. Is it true today?[9]

Taylorism is a dirty word to some, synonymous with mindless dehumanizing work. But if mass production developed along these lines, it was not Taylor's intent. His many innovations included

- Standardized work: Identifying the best and easiest way to do the job
  - Reduced cycle time: The time it takes for a given process
  - Time and motion study: A tool for developing standardized work
- Measurement and analysis to continually improve the process (a prototype of the plan-do-check-act cycle)

The great pioneers of Lean production, from Taiichi Ohno to Shigeo Shingo, have acknowledged their debt to Taylor.

Ford System

Meanwhile, a young entrepreneur named Henry Ford[10] was trying to design an automobile that was easy to manufacture and easy to repair. Ford finally achieved his goal with his 1908 Model T.

The key to mass production was not the assembly line. Rather, it was the thorough interchangeability of parts and ease of assembly. These innovations, in turn, made the assembly line possible. To achieve interchangeability Ford standardized gauge use throughout his operations. He was assisted by machine tool innovations that allowed machining of prehardened parts. This solved the warping that had confounded standardization.

Once parts could be standardized, design innovations followed. Ford reduced the number of moving parts in engines and other critical systems and simplified the assembly process. For example, Ford's engine casting comprised a single complex block. By contrast, competitors cast each cylinder individually and bolted them together.

These innovations resulted in huge savings. The need for part fitting, so expensive under craft production, was greatly reduced. Moreover, the goal of easy repair by the user became reachable.

The next problem was how to coordinate assembly. Assembly entailed a sequential series of dependent events. Once a given process was completed, the vehicle would be pulled to the next one. Such a system is unstable. Bottlenecks and other headaches were common as faster workers overtook slower ones.

To reduce such hassles, Ford started delivering parts to the work area, thus reducing the walk time of assembly workers. Moreover, following Taylor's lead, he reduced the number of actions each worker was required to do. Cycle times, which had measured in hours in 1908, dropped to a few minutes in 1913 at Ford's new Highland Park assembly plant.

There Ford hit upon the inspired idea of the moving assembly line that brought the car past the stationary worker. The assembly line reduced walk time and, most important, linked sequential processes. Thus, slower workers sped up and faster workers slowed down, achieving overall stability.

In summary, Ford's principal innovations during this period were

- Interchangeability and ease of assembly of parts
- Reduction of actions required of each worker
- Moving assembly line

These greatly reduced the amount of human effort required to assemble the vehicle. They also resulted in spectacular cost reductions. Ford was able to continually cut the price of the automobile as production volume soared. Between 1908 and the early 1920s, when Ford hit peak production of 2 million units per year, he had cut the real cost to the customer by two-thirds.[11] Womack has argued that Henry Ford was practicing Lean production at Highland Park, and that most manufacturers begin as Lean producers with one product.[12] It is only when they begin to produce multiple products that process villages, large batches, and other symptoms of mass production become evident.

Ford's system catapulted the company to industry leadership. The efficiencies released were such that Ford was famously able to double the wage of assembly workers to five dollars per day. The logical limit of the Ford system was the vast Rouge complex, which comprised a steel mill, casting plant, glass factory, metal forming and cutting operations, as well as the assembly operations.

HENRY AND EDSEL FORD—THE PRIDE AND THE SORROW[13]

Is there a more contradictory figure in American manufacturing history than Henry Ford? In his early years, a visionary inventor, entrepreneur, and philanthropist. In his later years, a paranoid, Nazi-appeasing bully.

His son Edsel, a gifted and visionary executive in his own right, bore the brunt of Henry's abuse. But when President Roosevelt called on American industry to become the "arsenal of democracy," it was Edsel who answered the call. In 1941, as Hitler's armies ran rampant, FDR realized he needed weaponry to fight the Nazis—most importantly, airplanes—and he needed them fast. When asked if Ford could deliver 50,000 airplanes, Edsel replied that Ford Motor Company would erect a plant that could produce a "bomber an hour!"

Critics scoffed: "Ford makes simple, affordable cars. They can't make planes!"

Defying his father, Edsel built the vast Willow Run plant, and brought in tens of thousands of workers from across the country. In a short time Edsel helped to transform Detroit from Motor City to the "great arsenal of democracy." Ford Motor Company would apply assembly-line mass production to build the American military's largest, fastest, and most destructive bomber, the B-24 Liberator. Mass production and the Ford system were crucial to the Allied victory. Without Edsel's vision and drive the war might have dragged on for years.

Ironically, the Ford system was later made obsolescent by Toyota and other challengers. So it goes. Each generation challenges the achievements of the last. But I can't help wondering: What if Edsel had lived? Would the Ford system have evolved quicker and been better able to meet the Toyota challenge?

We'll never know. But it's good to see Edsel Ford get due recognition. A talented and generous man, dealt a difficult hand, he played his cards with courage and vision. He is one of WWII's unsung heroes. Henry and Edsel remain the pride and sorrow of American manufacturing.

Other Developments

Two other developments also influenced the development of mass production:

- The managerial and marketing innovations of Alfred Sloan and General Motors
- The rise of the mass production labor movement

Sloan recognized that the mass production system required professional management. He decentralized GM's vast operations into five automobile divisions and a number of parts divisions. Each was run by a general manager, and reported to a small corporate headquarters. Each profit center used standard measures to report to senior management, which managed objectively, "by the numbers." Generally accepted accounting practice (GAAP) was developed to support this system.

Sloan's innovations greatly advanced management science. But again, there were unpleasant side effects:

- The gap between management and the shop floor was widened.
- Accounting practice came to encourage wasteful manufacturing practices such as building to inventory rather than customer demand.

Mass production also proved a fertile environment for a successful union movement. The division of labor resulted in meaningless, mind-numbing work. Workers, like machines, were considered to be interchangeable. Moreover, workers were considered a variable cost and could be jettisoned with any downturn of sales. After almost a decade of labor unrest, the United Auto Workers signed agreements with what had become the Big Three in the late 1930s.

These agreements recognized the respective roles of management and the union as well as the nature of mass production work. The main issues were job seniority and job rights. As sales went through their periodic downturns, workers were laid off in terms of seniority, not competence. Seniority also governed job assignments, the senior workers getting the easier jobs. This resulted in a never-ending battle over job rights and highly restrictive work rules that reduced the overall efficiency of the system. The polarization between management and the shop floor was complete.

This is traditional mass production. Take the Taylor system, add Ford's manufacturing innovations and Sloan's marketing and administrative techniques, and mix in organized labor's new role in controlling work tasks and job assignments. The system marched to victory after victory for decades. But there were signs of trouble.

Growing Dysfunction

Worker Alienation

Traditional mass production had its problems. Workers hated it: nobody wanted to be at the plant. Unions continually fought to reduce working hours. There was little sense of partnership between the company and its workers.

Indeed, it was more like trench warfare. Many works of art satirized mass production, including Charlie Chaplin's classic film, *Modern Times*.

Quality

Quality took a backseat to production, and defect rates were very high by current standards. Workers were not involved in the organization of the work. They routinely withheld information that might improve the process. End-of-line inspection became the norm. Quality specialists checked the finished products and an army of repair technicians fixed the substandard products.

Machinery

Machinery became larger and larger in pursuit of scale economies. Stamping machines, for example, often specialized in stamping a single part. To justify the massive expense of the machinery, the accounting profession developed cost accounting principles that emphasized unit, rather than overall, efficiency.

This encouraged batch production, and the buildup of huge work-in-progress and finished goods inventories (even if there were no customers to buy them). These appeared as assets on company balance sheets, despite the enormous amounts of cash they absorbed. The emphasis became to keep the machine running at all costs. Batch production also created quality problems: a defect would be replicated throughout the batch before it was caught. Hence, the so-called "move the metal" mentality that avoided line stoppages at any price and emphasized end-of-line repair by armies of specialists.

Engineering

Mass production also sowed the seeds of dysfunction in the engineering profession. Just as shop floor labor was minutely divided, so too was the work of engineers. As products became more and more complex, engineering branched into myriad specialities. Engineers had less and less to say to other engineers outside their subspecialties. This led to design problems: the less engineers talked to one another, the longer it took to bring a product from design to production.

Despite these problems, the mass production system rolled along. The United States dominated the manufacturing world. Mass production also diffused to Europe, first through the expansion of Ford and General Motors and later through the growth of companies such as Fiat, Renault, and Citroen.

This state of affairs might have continued indefinitely but for the oil crisis of the 1970s and developments in Toyota City.

THE HUMAN MIND LIKES BATCHES

When we were launching our coaching business we sent out a fair amount of mail. I asked Eleanor, my seven-year old, if she'd help with the stuffing, stamping, and labeling. She was thrilled.

"How do you think we should do it, my dear?"

"I think we should stuff all the letters first; then label them all; then seal them all; then stamp them all, Daddy."

"How about we do an experiment? You do them in batches, and I'll do them one at a time."

"OK, Dad."

Eleanor and I learned directly that one-at-a-time production is quicker and easier, even if it is counterintuitive.

Birth of Lean Production

In the spring of 1950, a young Japanese engineer named Eiji Toyoda visited Ford's vast Rouge plant in Detroit. Both Japan and the Toyota Motor Company, which his family had founded in 1937, were in crisis. After 13 years of effort Toyota had only been able to produce 2,685 automobiles. By contrast Ford's Rouge plant was producing 7,000 per day.[14]

Eiji Toyoda studied every corner of the Rouge, the world's biggest and most efficient manufacturing complex. Upon his return to Japan, Eiji and his production genius, Taiichi Ohno, concluded that mass production would not work in Japan. They also concluded, famously, that "there are some possibilities to improve the production system." This book describes the system they developed.

Toyota faced daunting challenges:

■ The domestic market was small and demanded a wide range of vehicles: large trucks to carry produce to markets, small trucks for farmers, luxury cars for the elite, and small cars suitable for Japan's narrow roads and high energy prices.

- The war-torn Japanese economy was starved for capital. Therefore, a huge investment in the latest Western technology was impossible.
- The outside world was full of established carmakers eager to establish themselves in Japan and to defend their markets against Japanese exports.

How could a fledgling carmaker in a ruined country surmount such obstacles?

MEETING EIJI TOYODA

Eiji Toyoda toured Toyota Motor Manufacturing Canada in 1996. He and his entourage dropped in to see our Health Center. I had heard that he was a tough old dude, and I was ready.

After the introductions he began to grill me. "How many visits to the Health Center every day? What are the most common types of injuries? What are your most serious long-term problems? What are you doing about them?"

Always checking.

Historic Bargain

Japan was in the throes of a depression. The occupying Americans had decided to attack inflation by restricting credit, but they overdid it. As car sales collapsed and its bank loans became exhausted, Toyota faced bankruptcy.

Toyota President Kiichiro Toyoda proposed firing a quarter of the workforce, a desperate measure. The company quickly found itself facing a major revolt. The company's union was in a strong bargaining position thanks to labor laws passed in 1946. The Japanese government, under American prompting, had strengthened the rights of unions and imposed severe restrictions on the ability of company owners to fire employees.[15]

After extended negotiations, the family and the union worked out a compromise:

1. A quarter of the workforce was terminated as originally proposed.
2. Kiichiro Toyoda resigned as president to take responsibility for the company's failure.

3. The remaining employees received two guarantees:
   a. Lifetime employment
   b. Pay steeply graded to seniority and tied to company profitability through bonuses

In addition, the employees received access to Toyota facilities including housing, recreation, and so forth. The employees also agreed to be flexible in work assignments and active in supporting the interests of the company by initiating improvement efforts.

The union and company had struck a historic bargain. In effect: "We will take you for life, but you have to do the work that needs doing, and you have to help us to improve." And thus, the workers became part of the Toyota community.

This remarkable agreement remains the model for labor relations in the Japanese automotive industry. It had deep implications:

1. The workers were now a fixed cost, like the company's machinery, more so, in fact, because machines could be depreciated. Therefore, the company had to get the most out of its human capital. It made sense to continually enhance the workers' skills and to gain benefits from their knowledge and experience.
2. It made sense for workers (or managers, who were covered by the agreement) to stay with the company. A 40-year-old at Toyota doing the same work as a 20-year-old received substantially higher wages. If the 40-year-old were to quit and join another company, he would have to start at the bottom of the pay scale.

EMPLOYMENT SECURITY AND INVOLVEMENT

At Toyota Cambridge we never worried about "kaizening" ourselves out of a job. Our policy was that a layoff would only be considered in the most extreme circumstances and as a last resort. Thus, team members felt secure enough to become involved in waste reduction activities. A virtuous cycle ensued: the more muda we eliminated, the greater was the demand for our products. The greater the demand was, the more we benefited (and the more involvement was required).

And so the foundation was created for an entirely different employment contract, one based on cooperation, flexibility, and mutual benefits. The company and the workers had become partners. The most important condition for Lean production had been established.

NUMMI: THE HISTORIC BARGAIN REPRISED[16]

In the early 1980s necessity brought Toyota and General Motors together in Fremont, California, in a joint venture called New United Motor Manufacturing Company (NUMMI). GM had to learn how to build high-quality and profitable small cars. Toyota, facing possible import restrictions, had to start building cars in the United States. Toyota also wanted to learn whether its manufacturing system would work with non-Japanese workers.

The NUMMI site had been built and operated by GM from 1962 to 1982. The plant and workforce were considered to be among GM's worst, infamous for sex, drugs, and bad cars. Employees drank and fought on the job. High absenteeism often stopped the production line. Workers were also known for sabotage such as putting "Coke bottles inside the door panels, so they'd rattle and annoy the customer."

Toyota took on the challenge under the following conditions: (1) Toyota would run the plant using the Toyota Production System, (2) almost all the troublesome GM workforce would be rehired, and (3) advance "commandos" would be sent to Japan to learn TPS.

In December 1984, the first car, a yellow Chevrolet Nova, rolled off the assembly line. Almost at once, NUMMI cars were as good as those produced in Japan, and NUMMI became one of GM's best factories.

Toyota, remarkably, also shared its production secrets with its partner. But GM would take another decade and a half to begin seriously implementing those lessons in its own factories. Some GM managers who worked at NUMMI saw the joint venture as a lost opportunity and wondered what might have been.

I was lucky enough to visit NUMMI many times and made friends both in management and the union. I remember a fine dinner in San Francisco with the president of the union local, who had been a troublemaker in the GM days.

"So what's really happening at NUMMI, Jim," I asked, "beneath all the lovey-dovey stuff?"

"The Japanese are tough," he replied, "but they're fair. The deal is: 'You do the work that needs doing, and help us to improve, and you'll have a job as long as you want it!' They really do want us to stop the line and fix quality problems. In fact, the president is concerned we're not stopping the line enough! He asked for my help with it."

A Novel Concept

Taiichi Ohno already knew that workers were his most valuable resource. Withholding of information or ideas, so common in the mass production plants, would rapidly lead to disaster in the fledgling Toyota system. In the years to come, Ohno and his team developed activities to fully involve team members in improvement, an utterly novel idea.

TAYLOR AND OHNO

Fred Taylor separated planning and production; Taiichi Ohno brought them back together. It's easy to portray the former as villain and the latter as hero. But history is ironic. Ohno repeatedly cited his debt to Taylor. Indeed, his fledgling Toyota system depended on Taylor's ideas: time and motion studies, standardized work, and continuous improvement. And Ohno's system expressed Taylor's deepest hopes for a harmonious, humane workplace.

A Virtue of Necessity

The Toyota Production System, or Lean production, was the solution to Toyota's problems. Over the next 30 years, Taiichi Ohno solved these problems one by one, and pushed his system through Toyota. Like any change agent, Ohno faced daunting obstacles, but he had a few things going for him. He was a genius, he was obnoxious, and he had Eiji Toyoda's support.

The ensuing chapters of this book examine the innovations that Ohno and his team developed. In each case they made a virtue of necessity. And each step forward depended on the skill and creativity of shop floor team members.

For example, Ohno's budget precluded the purchase of the enormous machines common in North America. Dedicating a stamping machine to a single part, for instance, as was common in the Big Three, was out of the question. Instead, Toyota had to stamp multiple parts from each machine. This meant smaller batches and quick die[17] changeovers. Ohno's workers invented quick die changeover. Where a changeover could take a day or longer at a typical mass producer, Toyota's workers could do it in a matter of minutes.

Remarkably, Ohno found that producing smaller batches with quick changeovers actually resulted in cost savings. Small batches also improved quality because defects could be detected more quickly and reduced lead times because there was less work-in-process. Many of his subsequent discoveries also proved to be counterintuitive.

At Toyota I came to understand that our problems today are those Toyota faced in 1950:

- Fragmented markets demanding many products in low volumes
- Tough competition
- Fixed or falling prices
- Rapidly changing technology
- High cost of capital
- Capable workers demanding higher levels of involvement

But today we have a map and a compass.

Completing the Lean Revolution at Toyota

By the late 1960s Taiichi Ohno had pushed his innovations through Toyota's production facilities. The next step was for Toyota's suppliers to implement the Lean system. In 1969, Ohno established the Production Research Office (now called the Operations Management Consulting Division, OMCD) to set up joint working groups among Toyota's largest and most important

IS THE LEAN SYSTEM JAPANESE?

Lean production is not the norm in Japan. Most Japanese manufacturers struggle with the same difficulties that we face in North America. Not long ago I spoke at a Lean production conference that was covered by a Japanese TV news crew. I asked the producer about the current events in Japan. She said that there was much soul-searching, and the sense that the country had lost its way. Japan had not embraced manufacturing excellence, she suggested, but had been seduced by the bubble economy.

suppliers. Six groups of seven were established, each with a team leader. Each group was asked to conduct one major kaizen per month with the assistance of OMCD. The executives of the other groups reviewed the results and made suggestions. Toyota compelled the transformation by demanding continual price reductions in part costs every year. In this way the Toyota system permeated the entire supply chain by the end of the 1970s.[18]

OMCD continues to serve as a consulting group to Toyota plants and suppliers around the world. In 1993 Ohno protégé Hajime Ohba became general manager of the Toyota Supplier Support Center (TSSC) in Lexington, Kentucky. TSSC teaches Lean thinking to American firms, many of them neither Toyota suppliers, nor in the auto sector.

WHY LEAN OUTSIDE THE FACTORY?

Lean is about reducing waste and variation, and much of it is outside the factory. In the past few decades, factories have greatly improved, and in some industries are no longer the bottleneck. For example, our family purchased a Toyota Avalon last year, a splendid vehicle built at the Toyota Kentucky factory. Total lead time between our order and vehicle delivery was 31 days. But the vehicle only spent a day or so in the factory!

Even at Toyota, the greatest opportunities for improvement often lie in areas such as sales, marketing, design, purchasing, and engineering. These, as well as industries including healthcare, financial services, education, and public service are Lean's "undiscovered country."

Summary

Fred Taylor and Henry Ford sought to address the weaknesses of craft production. Taylor's scientific management and Ford's factory innovations laid the foundation for mass production. Alfred Sloan's managerial innovations and the role of organized labor in controlling work tasks and job assignments completed the system. Mass production rolled to victory after victory for decades.

Toyota faced daunting financial, technological, and labor relations challenges 50 years ago. Eiji Toyoda concluded that mass production would not work in Japan. He and his production genius, Taiichi Ohno, created a system that made a virtue of necessity. For example, the unavailability of capital spurred the development of flexible, right-sized machinery, and quick changeovers. The legal restrictions on worker layoffs created the image of the company as community and laid the foundation for intense employee involvement and problem solving.

It took Ohno 30 years to perfect his system and drive it through Toyota. He set up the Operations Management Consulting Division (OMCD) to support Lean thinking in Toyota plants and suppliers. The system would have been remarkable under any circumstances. But today we face the same daunting problems that Toyota faced half a century ago. Ohno's system is more relevant than ever.

Reference

Pascal Dennis, *The Remedy: Bringing Lean Thinking Out of the Factory to Transform the Entire Organization* (New York: Wiley & Sons, 2010).

Endnotes

1. A.J. Baime, *The Arsenal of Democracy* (New York: Houghton Mifflin Harcourt, 2014).
2. I am indebted to James Womack, Daniel Jones, and Daniel Roos, authors of *The Machine That Changed the World*; and to Toyota City for *Toyota: A History of the First 50 Years* (New York: Simon & Schuster, 1990) upon which much of this chapter is based.
3. Toyota Motor Corporation, *Toyota: A History of the First 50 Years* (Toyota City, 1988).
4. James Womack, Daniel Jones, and Daniel Roos, *The Machine That Changed the World* (New York: Simon & Schuster, 1990).
5. Toyota Motor Corporation, Operations Management Consulting Division, *The Toyota Production System* (Tokyo, 1995).
6. Robert Kanigel, *The One Best Way: Frederick Winslow Taylor and the Enigma of Efficiency* (Cambridge, MA: MIT Press, 2005).
7. Frederick Taylor, *Scientific Management* (New York: McGraw-Hill, 1908).
8. At the time, virtually all trades workers were male.
9. Evidently, the average IQ is rising across North America as people take advantage of the Internet and educational TV.
10. I use the automotive industry to illustrate essential manufacturing developments in the twentieth century. I do not wish to minimize the importance of developments in other industries. Indeed, there were parallel developments and cross-fertilization.

11. James Womack, Daniel Jones, and Daniel Roos, *The Machine That Changed the World* (New York: Simon & Schuster, 1990).
12. James Womack, "The Challenge of Value Stream Management," *Value Stream Management Conference*, Dearborn, MI, December 2000.
13. A.J. Baime, *The Arsenal of Democracy* (New York: Houghton Mifflin Harcourt, 2014).
14. James Womack, "The Challenge of Value Stream Management," *Value Stream Management Conference*, Dearborn, MI, December 2000.
15. Ironically, in Japan, General MacArthur was able to implement the progressive labor legislation that President Roosevelt had failed to implement in the United States.
16. National Public Radio, "NUMMI Plant Closure Ends Toyota-GM Joint Venture" http://www.npr.org/templates/story/story.php?storyId=125430405
17. A die is a piece of hard metal used to shape sheet metal. Stamping machines create desired shapes out of sheet metal "blanks" by bringing matched upper and lower dies together under thousands of pounds of pressure.
18. James Womack, "The Challenge of Value Stream Management," *Value Stream Management Conference*, Dearborn, MI, December, 2000.

Study Questions

1. Can you think of a contemporary industry or profession that employs craft production principles?
   a. What are the strengths of this industry or profession?
   b. What are the weaknesses?
   c. What are the biggest threats it faces?
   d. What do you think this industry or profession needs to do to improve?
2. Can you think of an industry or profession that employs mass production principles?
   a. What are the strengths of this industry or profession?
   b. What are its weaknesses?
   c. What are the biggest threats it faces?
   d. What do you think this industry or profession needs to do to improve?
3. During the past five years, Toyota has faced its worst crisis in 50 years.
   a. How has Toyota responded to the crisis?
   b. What do you think is the root cause of Toyota's crisis?
   c. What do you think is the correct countermeasure?
   d. What countermeasures has Toyota taken? Do you think they will be effective? Explain your answers.
   e. Any reflections or learning points?

Chapter 2

Lean Production System

Adopt the new philosophy...we are in a new economic age.

W. Edwards Deming

Lean production, also known as the Toyota Production System, means doing more with less—less time, less space, less human effort, less machinery, less materials—while giving customers what they want. Two important books popularized the term "Lean":

- *The Machine That Changed the World*, by James Womack, Daniel Jones, and Daniel Roos and published by Simon & Schuster in 1990
- *Lean Thinking*, by James Womack and Daniel Jones, published by Simon & Schuster in 1996

Although Lean principles are rooted in manufacturing, I have found that they apply universally. Our challenge is to translate, tailor, and apply them to our particular situation.

Why Lean Production?

New Economics

It used to be that companies could set their prices according to the following formula:[1,2]

$$Cost + Profit\ margin = Price$$

The accounting department would determine cost based on the principles of cost accounting and a profit margin typical for the industry would be added. The price would be passed on to the customer, who, more often than not, paid it.

This is no longer true. The profit equation is now as follows:

$$\text{Price (fixed)} - \text{Cost} = \text{Profit}$$

In most industries, price is fixed (or falling). Customers are more powerful than ever before. They have a wealth of choices, unprecedented access to information, and demand excellent quality at a reasonable price.

In such an environment, the only way to improve profit is to reduce cost. The great challenge of the twenty-first century is not information technology. It is cost reduction. Can your company continually improve quality and enlarge customer choices while reducing cost? Figure 2.1[3] summarizes these ideas.

But we must reduce cost without

- Decimating our team members
- Cannibalizing our maintenance budgets
- Weakening our company in the long term

In fact, the only sustainable way of reducing cost is to involve your team members in improvement. How to motivate involvement? How to win the hearts and minds of your people?

The Toyota system relentlessly attacks *muda* (waste) by involving team members in shared, standardized improvement activities. A virtuous cycle ensues: the more team members are involved, the more success they enjoy. The more success they enjoy, the greater are the intrinsic and extrinsic rewards, which stimulates more involvement, and so on.

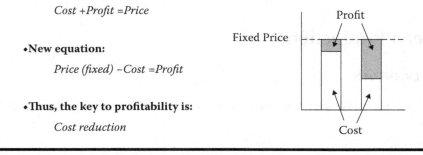

•**Old equation:**

    Cost +Profit =Price

•**New equation:**

    Price (fixed) –Cost =Profit

•**Thus, the key to profitability is:**

    Cost reduction

Figure 2.1　The goal is cost reduction.

Benefits go directly to the bottom line.

■ Old equation:

$$Cost + Profit = Price$$

■ New equation:

$$Price\ (fixed) - Cost = Profit$$

■ Thus, the key to profitability:
  Cost reduction

BRIGADOON

Apparently, there are still organizations that can pass price increases on to the customer with impunity. These include government agencies, cartels supported by government, companies with proprietary technology, or companies engaged in monkey business.

Systems and Systems Thinking

A system is an integrated series of parts with a clearly defined goal. For example, a car is a system whose goal is to provide transportation. Systems have the following characteristics:[4]

■ Each part of a system has a definable purpose. For example, the purpose of a car engine is to provide motive force.
■ The parts of the system are interdependent. A car engine depends on the fuel subsystem to provide chemical energy and the transmission subsystem to make the wheels spin.
■ We can understand each part by seeing how it fits into the system. But we cannot understand the system by identifying the unassembled parts. What makes a car cannot be found in the parts—after all, a helicopter also has an engine, fuel system, and transmission—but in how the parts fit together.
■ To understand the system we must understand its purpose, its interdependencies, and its interactions. A car's engine may be working fine, but if the transmission column is detached, the car won't move. In other words, we must learn to think in terms of wholes as well as parts.

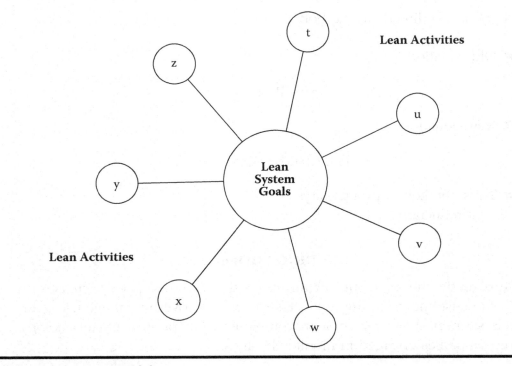

Figure 2.2 System model.

The solar system model, which I introduced in an earlier book,[5] is a simple system picture and is shown in Figure 2.2. The "sun" or heart of the system is our goals and objectives. The "planets" are the activities or components of the system, which we will use to achieve our goals. The closer the activity is to the "sun," the greater is its importance in achieving our goals. When developing systems, it is wise to prioritize our activities (A, B, C) and build accordingly.

But our system models are just pictures. To understand a system and to make it real, we have to link our model to actual practice. Figure 2.3 shows the link between our system model and actual practice. Activities *tuvwxyz* in the system model must be translated into actions *TUVWXYZ* on the shop floor. And our understanding of Lean system A, our mental model, must be translated into Lean system B, the reality on the shop floor. These are difficult tasks in a fast-paced manufacturing environment.

Systems thinking[6] is the ability to think in terms of systems and knowing how to lead systems. Systems thinking is difficult. Evolution has programmed us to react to immediate threats. Our nervous system is focused on dramatic external events such as sharp noises and sudden changes in our visual field. We are poorly prepared for a world of slowly developing threats.

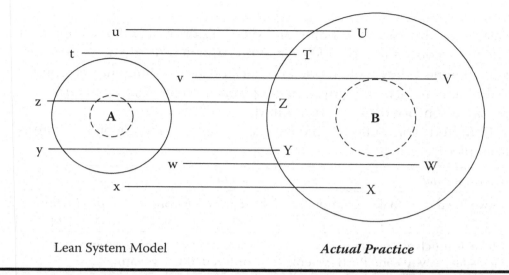

Lean System Model   *Actual Practice*

Figure 2.3   System model and actual practice.

BEGINNER'S MIND

One of the nice things about Toyota manufacturing offices is that there are no walls, literally. Therefore, one is able to ask smart people basic questions.

I once asked a Toyota executive to tell me the plan-do-check-act cycle.

He responded: "Ah, PDCA. It took me ten years to learn plan, ten years for do, and ten years each for check and act. Now I begin to understand PDCA."

The "Thinking Way"

Lean *senseis* (ones who have gone before) emphasize the "thinking way."[7] Everything else can be taught. But how can we deepen our thinking? How can we develop richer mental models?[8] Through self-awareness and endless practice.[9] Think of a samurai warrior polishing his blade, hence, the *do*, or path concept (which is discussed further in Chapter 9).

MENTAL MODELS

Mental models are one's expectations about how the world works based on temperament, upbringing, and experience. Mental models are the glasses we all wear, which filter and often distort reality. For example, at a dentists' convention, people look at one another's teeth; at a chiropractic conference, they look at one another's posture—different perceptions of the same reality. Similarly, two people go into the same party, pick up the same sensory data, but pick out different faces.

Lean and "conventional" mental models differ fundamentally. Here is a sample:

Conventional	Toyota/Lean
Move the metal! Make your numbers!	Stop production, so that production never has to stop! (Jidoka concept)
Make as much as you can. Go as fast as you can. (Push system)	Make only what the customer has ordered. (Pull system)
Make big batches and move them slowly through the system. (Batch and queue)	Make things one at a time and move them quickly through the system. (Flow)
Thou shalt! (Leader = Boss)	What do you think? (Leader = Teacher)
We have some standards. (Not sure where they are or if they're followed)	We have simple visual standards for all important things.
Engineers and other specialists create standards. The rest of us do what we're told.	The people closest to the work develop standards and pull in specialists as required.
Don't get caught holding the bag!	Make problems visible.
Only grunts go to the shop floor.	Go and see for yourself.
Do-Do-Do-Do!	Plan-Do-Check-Act (PDCA)

In the chapters to come, see if you can identify the underlying Lean mental models and how they differ from conventional thinking.

Basic Image of Lean Production

Taiichi Ohno conceived the Lean system. It has been extended and deepened by a series of outstanding practitioners, including

- Hiroyuki Hirano: 5S system
- Seiichi Nakajima: Total productive maintenance (TPM)

- Kenichi Sekine: Continuous flow
- Shigeo Shingo: Jidoka and single-minute exchange of dies (SMED)

However, the Lean system has proven difficult to grasp as a whole. The tendency has been to cherry-pick activities—a smattering of 5S, a kaizen blitz, some TPM—which has failed to produce the desired results. Such implementation efforts, at their worst, seem a Frankenstein, a project made up of various ill-fitting parts, stitched together in the hope that something will bring it to life. At Toyota, by contrast, I found that our efforts proceeded organically, guided by the question: What is the need?

The books of Taiichi Ohno and of Professor Yasuhiro Monden of the University of Tsukuba are invaluable resources that describe Toyota in detail. However, their depth and scope tend to overwhelm the newcomer to Lean production. To extend the Indian metaphor of the blind men and the elephant, which I introduced earlier, these books are for people who already know what elephants look like and who wish to learn more about their mating habits, social structure, and blood chemistry, as opposed to people who have no direct experience with elephants and just want to know what they look like. Moreover, Mr. Ohno's aphorisms have a Zen aspect, which may not be familiar to many non-Toyota readers.

The excellent books of Jim Womack and Dan Jones have deepened our appreciation of the Toyota system and have placed it in a social and historical context. Womack and Jones continue to break new ground. But their work is not aimed at the shop floor practitioner.

A picture is worth a thousand words. The House of Lean Production, shown in Figure 2.4, is our picture.[10,11] It has taken me years to grasp. In the chapters to come we review each part of the house. As your understanding deepens, you will perceive layers of meaning and come to understand the importance of a humble spirit.

The foundation of the Lean system is stability and standardization. The walls are just-in-time delivery of parts of products and *jidoka*, or automation with a human mind. The goal (the roof) of the system is customer focus: to deliver the highest quality to the customer, at the lowest cost, in the shortest lead time. The heart of the system is involvement: flexible, motivated team members continually seeking a better way.

At Toyota I came to understand that each activity is interconnected and that the same "thinking way" informs them. The power of the Toyota system is in the continual reinforcement of core concepts. Figure 2.5 illustrates

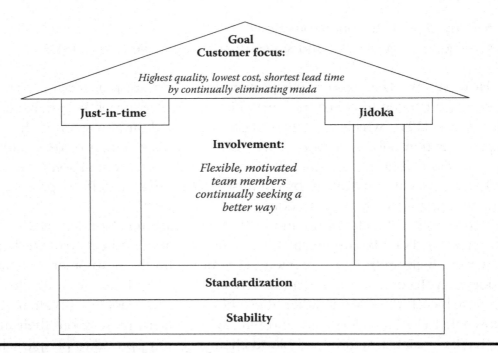

Figure 2.4 Basic image of Lean production.

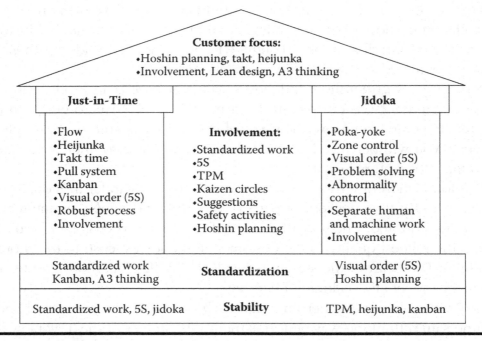

Figure 2.5 Lean activities.

where the various Lean activities fit. In the ensuing chapters we illustrate each component of our image.

WHAT IS VALUE?

If we get value wrong, everything goes wrong. It's our alpha and omega. By definition, work is *motion that creates value*. So what is *value*?

Let's begin by asking

1. Who are our customers, both internal and external?
2. What do they need from us? (What do they value?)

In some cases, the answers come relatively easily. Suppose, for example, that we're the paint shop in an auto plant. We usually understand our external customer, the buyer, and internal customer, the downstream process: assembly. We know what they want from us and are able to define a handful of corresponding metrics.

But what if we're an internal support group that doesn't deal directly with the external customer, and has multiple internal customers? Suppose, for example, that we're the blood bank in a major hospital:

1. Who are our customers?
   a. Operating rooms
   b. Emergency department
   c. Other
2. What do they need from us?
   This one requires considerable back and forth discussion. With time, we could translate each customer's needs into specific targets for
   a. Blood plasma volume
   b. Blood mix
   c. Turnaround times
   d. Quality

Now let's put those up on our team board, and hold a daily huddle wherein we ask

■ How are we doing with respect to our targets?
■ What are our top three problems?

- What are we doing about them?
- What else can we do to improve?
- How do we involve more people in improvement work?

We're in the game.

Customer Focus

Our core goal is to provide the highest quality, at the lowest cost, in the shortest time by continually eliminating muda or waste. But today customers have broader expectations. Thus, Lean companies have added safety, environment, and morale to their core goals. Hence, the acronym PQCDSM:

- Productivity
- Quality
- Cost
- Delivery time
- Safety and environment
- Morale

We must confirm on a daily basis that our activities are advancing PQCDSM. Otherwise, it's pure muda.

DEFINING VALUE REQUIRES FINESSE

Value is like a diamond. Hold it up to the light and a range of colors emerges. Not all are relevant to our situation. Here are some common definitions:

1. Value is what the customer is willing to pay for.

   A helpful definition, with some pitfalls. Clearly, customers don't want to pay for waste. But how well does the customer understand waste? And often the customer has no consciousness of *unmet needs*. For example, before Steve Jobs and the Apple team developed the iPad, did customers know they needed, wanted, and would delight in it? Similarly, what is value for a design team? Our external customer would have little idea. They might consider continuous experimentation and the culling of failed designs as "waste." But this is how a design team creates value!

2. Value is an activity that changes the form, fit, or function of a product.

   A manufacturing definition. Does it have any meaning for, say, a hospital, bank, or community college?

3. Value = Quality/Cost.

   A broadly serviceable definition.

Value must also be felt *viscerally*. We need a direct relationship with the customer so we can translate their needs into a simple binary metrics that we can put on our team boards. Inviting customers to team huddles is a great way of maintaining the connection.

Muda

Muda is the one Japanese word you must know. It is just what it sounds like. Heavy and foul, it sticks in your mouth. Muda means waste, or any activity for which the customer is not willing to pay.[12]

Muda is the opposite of value, which is simply what a customer is willing to pay for. Consider a filing cabinet manufacturer. The customer is willing to pay for sheet metal to be cut, bent, welded, and painted. But the customer is not willing to pay for wait time, rework, or excess inventory or any of the other forms of muda.

Human motion can be divided into three categories (Figure 2.6):[13,14]

- Actual work: Refers to any motion that adds value to the product or service.
- Auxiliary work: Motion that supports actual work; usually occurs before or after the actual work (e.g., picking a part out of a supplier's box or setting the part in a machine).
- Muda: Motion that creates no value. Here is a good test: if you stopped doing this, there would be no adverse effect on the product.

Consider a spot welding operation:

- Actual work comprises those few moments of spot welding.
- Auxiliary work might comprise setting up and removing the work piece.

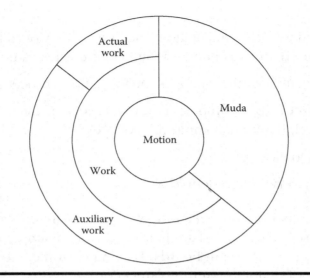

Figure 2.6 Work versus muda.

- ■ Muda might comprise:
  - – Unnecessary walking or reaching to set up the work piece
  - – Making more spot welds than necessary
  - – Making more pieces than the customer demands

There are eight different kinds of muda, as shown in Figure 2.7.[15] Also shown is the remarkable 5/95 ratio of value to muda common in most operations. Most of our day-to-day activity is muda. Hence Taiichi Ohno's great line: "True cost is the size of a plum seed."

But this also represents a tremendous opportunity. Think of waste as a bank account full of our money. We need to learn how to make withdrawals.

Motion

Wasted motion has both a human and machine element. Wasted human motion is related to workplace ergonomics. Poor ergonomic design negatively affects productivity and quality as well as safety. Productivity suffers when there is unnecessary walking, reaching, or twisting. Quality suffers when the worker has to strain to process or check the work piece because of reaching, twisting, or poor environmental conditions.

Poor ergonomics has perhaps the biggest impact on safety. Ergonomic injuries comprise more than 50% of all workplace injuries in North America. The most important ergonomic risk factors are posture, force, and repetition,

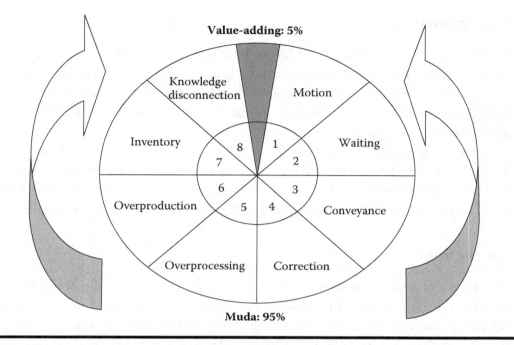

Figure 2.7   Learning to see muda.

all of which depend on workplace design. Ergonomics, therefore, is a key to reducing the muda of human motion.

Delay

Waiting waste occurs when a worker has to wait for material to be delivered, or for a line stoppage to be cleared, or when employees stand around waiting for a machine to process a part. It also occurs when there is excessive work-in-process (WIP) because of large batch production, equipment problems downstream, or defects requiring rework.

Delays increase lead time—that is, the time between the customer placing and receiving his or her order—a critical measure in the Lean system. Lead time may be defined as follows:

$$\text{Lead time} = \text{Processing time} + \text{Retention time}$$

Delays increase retention time, which far exceeds processing time in most manufacturing operations.

Conveyance

Conveyance waste includes the large-scale waste caused by inefficient work-place layout, overly large equipment, or traditional batch production. Such waste occurs, for example, when large batches must be moved from process to process. Making smaller batch sizes and moving processes closer together can reduce conveyance muda.

There is also a microcomponent related to work pieces being carried within a process area either by conveyor or by workers. Conveyance, delay, and motion wastes are closely related. Conveyance is necessary muda: obviously materials must be moved through the factory, but it must be minimized.

Correction

The muda of correction is related to making and having to fix defective products. It comprises all material, time, and energy involved in making and repairing defects. There is now a large body of literature on quality costs, that is, on the costs of correcting this muda.

Overprocessing

This is a subtle form of muda related to doing more than what the customer requires. Such muda often exists in companies driven by their engineering departments. For example, companies enamored of a given technology, or committed to achieving a certain technical goal, may lose touch with what the customer actually wants.

Porsche suffered from this in the 1980s as the company continually pursued engineering goals that were unrelated to the customer's desires. For example, Porsche automobiles of that era achieved incremental performance improvements at 200 km/h or more. But try changing the oil.

Inventory

The muda of inventory is related to the keeping of unnecessary raw materials, parts, and WIP. These conditions result when flow is constricted in a plant and when production is not linked to the drumbeat of the market (pull).

For example, organizations that schedule production solely on the basis of material requirement planning (MRP) systems inevitably have substantial muda of inventory. MRP is a "push" system. That is, production is scheduled at each department—or pushed along—regardless of the needs of the downstream process. These schedules are based on the inventory and WIP levels recorded in the database, which usually vary widely from actual levels. Thus, workers and supervisors make extra, "just in case," and WIP accumulates.

Overproduction

Taiichi Ohno saw overproduction as the root of all manufacturing evil.[16] Overproduction means making things that don't sell. Here are some of the related costs:

- Building and maintenance of large warehouses
- Extra workers and machines
- Extra parts and materials
- Extra energy, oil, and electricity
- Extra forklifts, tow trucks, pallets, and skids
- Extra interest payments on loans
- Hidden problems and invisible kaizen points

Overproduction is a root cause of other kinds of muda:

- *Motion:* Workers are busy making things that nobody ordered.
- *Waiting:* Related to large batch sizes.
- *Conveyance:* Unneeded finished goods must be moved to storage warehouses.
- *Correction:* Early detection of defects is more difficult with large batches.
- *Inventory:* Overproduction creates unnecessary raw materials, parts, and WIP.

If we prevent overproduction we will make major strides toward our goals.

Knowledge

This form of muda exists when there are disconnects within a company, or between the company and its customers and suppliers. Disconnects within a company can be horizontal, vertical, or temporal. These inhibit the flow of knowledge, ideas, and creativity, creating frustration and missed opportunities. The popularity of Dilbert suggests that knowledge waste may be at epidemic proportions in North America.

When a company is connected to the voice of the customer it will create products that consistently satisfy and even delight. When a company and its suppliers are in tune, they will jointly identify muda and act to their mutual benefit. There will be few missed opportunities. Womack and Jones[17] have coined the term "macro value stream" to highlight the opportunities that exist both upstream and downstream in the value chain.

A Word of Caution

Learning to see waste is an important first step. But the Lean system is much more than a scavenger hunt for muda. We also have important positive goals. For instance, we seek to create continuous flow so that the customer can pull. We seek to create stability so that any impediment to flow is readily apparent. We seek to employ the techniques of visual management so that the out-of-standard condition is visible. And we seek to involve our team members in all these activities because they are the wellspring of continuous improvement.

VALUE AT THE IMPERIAL GRILL

I grew up in a Greek restaurant, the Imperial Grill, a family diner on Toronto's Queen Street East. I love restaurants; they're the most basic kind of factory. The Imperial Grill was a Lean enterprise, and my folks, Frank and Helen, Lean thinkers, though they would simply call it common sense. I can hear my father's booming voice, "This is news? Of course you take care of customers! Of course you don't waste anything! Of course you keep inventory low! Any idiot knows that!"

My folks had a visceral understanding of value. What did customers expect of the Imperial Grill? Good food at fair prices, to be sure. But they also expected a warm accepting atmosphere, where they could kibitz with Mama, Uncle Louie, and the rest of the crew.

Value requires embedded tests that give you immediate OK/Not OK feedback. I remember my dad looking into the plates as they came back. Did the customers eat everything? If not, what did they leave behind, and why? Often he'd ask for direct feedback.

"Hey, Mabel, you didn't eat your moussaka! You don't like it?"

"Oh, no, Frankie, it was delicious! But it was more than I could eat."

"But you liked it! OK, Spyro, wrap it up for the lady. She'll have it for dinner!"

I saw the same kind of direct personal connections at our old plant, Toyota Motor Manufacturing Canada (TMMC), in the daily meetings between internal suppliers and customers.

"How'd we do today, Freddie?"

"Not bad, Rachel, except for excess sealer and weld burrs in the usual places, four and six of each, respectively. You know they affect how the quarter glass sets, which means ergonomic problems and water leaks. How's that kaizen coming?"

Value was clearly understood by both supplier and customer. Value was direct and personal: Freddie and Rachel having a stand-up meeting every day, binary embedded tests telling us whether we were OK/Not OK, and focused action on abnormalities.

How do you get people to care in this manner? This may be a leader's biggest challenge.

My folks ran the Imperial Grill for 40 years. They provided good food at fair prices and a warm accepting atmosphere, and put three kids through college. We lost my dad a few years ago (http://blog.lean systems.org/2013/08/in-memory-of-my-dad.html). My most poignant metaphor for value, and connection, remains Dad looking into the plate and asking Mabel why she didn't eat her moussaka.

Mura

Mura[18] refers to unevenness or fluctuation in work, usually caused by fluctuating production plans. A simple example might be a production line that is producing difficult models for half the shift and simple models for the second half, so that workers strain for half the day and coast the other half. The Lean system seeks to reduce mura through heijunka, or production leveling, by mixing models, for example.

Problem: How best to move 6000 kg load with a forklift having a capacity of 2000 kg?

Muda (waste): 6 trips @ 1000 kg

Mura (unevenness): 2 trips @ 2000 kg
2 trips @ 1000 kg

Muri (hard to do): 2 trips @ 3000 kg

Best: 3 trips @ 2000 kg

Load: 6000 kg   Capacity: 2000 kg

Figure 2.8   Muda, mura, and muri.[20]

Muri

Muri[19] means "hard to do" and can be caused by variations in production, poor job design or ergonomics, poor part fit, inadequate tools or jigs, unclear specifications, and so on.

Figure 2.8 illustrates the relationship between muda, mura, and muri.

Summary

I have introduced the House of Lean Production around which the book is organized. A central goal of the Lean system is to eliminate waste so as to improve profitability, the only effective strategy under the new economics. Lean activities are interrelated and mutually supportive and are informed by the same way of thinking.

The eight different kinds of muda or waste are discussed, as are the related concepts of mura and muri. Overproduction is the most serious waste. But Lean production is more than a scavenger hunt for muda. The positive goals of Lean production include creating flow so that the customer can pull and involving our workers in improvement activities.

Endnotes

1. Japanese Management Association, *Kanban—Just-in-Time at Toyota* (New York: Productivity Press, 1989).

2. Toyota Motor Corporation, Operations Management Consulting Division, *The Toyota Production System* (Tokyo, 1995).

3. Ibid.

4. Peter R. Scholtes, *The Leader's Handbook* (New York: McGraw-Hill, 1998), p. 21.

5. Pascal P. Dennis, *Quality Safety & Environment: Synergy in the 21st Century* (Milwaukee: ASQ Quality Press, 1997).

6. Peter Senge, *The Fifth Discipline* (New York: Doubleday, 1990).

7. Discussion with Toyota executive.

8. For a detailed discussion of Lean mental models, see Pascal Dennis, *Getting the Right Things Done: A Leader's Guide to Planning and Execution* (Cambridge, MA: LEI Press, 2006).

9. Shunryu Suzuki, *Zen Mind: Beginner's Mind* (New York: Weatherhill, 1970).

10. Japanese Management Association, *Kanban—Just-in-Time at Toyota* (New York: Productivity Press, 1989).

11. Toyota training document.

12. Japanese Management Association, *Kanban—Just-in-Time at Toyota* (New York: Productivity Press, 1989).

13. Toyota training document.

14. Toyota Motor Corporation, Operations Management Consulting Division, *The Toyota Production System* (Tokyo, 1995).

15. Toyota training document.

16. Taiichi Ohno, *Toyota Production System: Beyond Large Scale Production* (New York: Productivity Press, 1988).

17. James P. Womack and Daniel T. Jones, *Lean Thinking* (New York: Simon & Schuster, 1996).

18. Toyota training document.

19. Toyota training document.

20. Toyota training document.

Study Questions

1. Define value for the following organizations:
    a. Weld department in a truck manufacturing factory
    b. Purchasing department in an auto plant
    c. Quality department in a large appliance manufacturing plant
    d. Emergency department in a large urban hospital
    e. Mortgage department in a large bank
    f. Human resources department in a university
    g. Sales department in a home building company

In developing your answers for each, consider the following questions: Who are the customers? What do they need?

2. Provide at least one example of the eight kinds of waste for each of the following:
    a. Weld department in a truck manufacturing factory
    b. Purchasing department in an auto plant
    c. Quality department in a large appliance manufacturing plant
    d. Emergency department in a large urban hospital
    e. Mortgage department in a large bank
    f. Human resources department in a university
    g. Sales department in a home building company
3. Define value for your team.
    a. What are your team's critical few metrics?
    b. How well do they align with value?
    c. What might your team do to improve?
4. Provide at least one example of the eight kinds of waste for your team and/or work area.
    a. What are the most important forms of waste for your team or work area?
5. Provide at least three examples of *mura* (unevenness) and *muri* (strain) for your team or work area.
    a. What are causes of *mura* and *muri* for your team and/or work area?

Chapter 3

Stability

Give me a place to stand, and I can move the earth.

Archimedes

At Toyota I learned that improvement was impossible without stability in the 4 Ms:[1]

Man/woman
Machine
Material
Method

To stabilize we occasionally had to take non-Lean action such as increasing buffers or adding people or equipment. Such action bought us time so that we could solve our root problems while meeting our obligations to our internal and external customers.

Stability starts with visual management and the 5S system. 5S supports standardized work and total productive maintenance (TPM), which are key to method and machine stability, respectively.[2] Finally, 5S supports just-in-time (JIT) production by providing point-of-use information that eases decision making.

Lean System Standards

The bedrock of production is standards: what is supposed to happen. The bedrock of excellence is adherence to standards. Yet for many, the term *standard* connotes thick manuals of unreadable dreck. Government statutes are a good example.[3] I have a lawyer friend who jokes that he never reads statutes; it would kill his quality of life.

LEAN IMPROVEMENT PROCESS

At Toyota we learned simple, elegant improvement processes:

1. *Stabilize the 4 Ms:* You can't flow or pull unless you have stable manpower, methods, machines, and materials. Please focus on the biggest problems.
2. *Flow:* That is, as you stabilize, gradually reduce batch sizes and queue lengths. The ideal condition is to "make one—move one" (or "serve one—move one"). Doing so will lower operating expense (e.g., inventory cost), defects, and lead time.
3. *Pull:* That is, don't make one until the downsteam customer wants it. The magic of pull is in the control of work-in-process, which brings the benefits noted above.
4. *Improve the system:* We seek perfection, even though we know we'll never achieve it. Taiichi Ohno's insight cited in the last chapter, "True cost is the size of a plum seed," reflects this understanding. Our spirit should be humble but resolute. Each day we get a little better and we never give up.

I found standards to be very different at Toyota. Let us answer a few fundamental questions:[4]

1. What is a standard?
   – A standard is a clear image of a desired condition.
2. Why are standards so important in the Lean system?
   – Standards make abnormalities immediately obvious so that corrective action can be taken.
3. What makes an effective standard?
   – A good standard is simple, clear, and visual.

STANDARDS—A BASIS FOR COMPARISON

In Japanese, the term "standard" is free of the negative connotations noted above. A standard is a basis for comparison, a way of making the out-of-standard condition obvious so we can make countermeasures. Thus, a standard can be

- A one-page standardized work chart showing how to start the gas chromatograph in a laboratory
- A painted silhouette on a wall in a hospital maintenance shop, showing what jigs and tools belong there
- A delivery schedule board on a receiving dock showing what deliveries are expected and which ones have arrived on time
- A visual display in a new product development department showing the department's capacity, throughput and cycle time targets, current project load, and what phase each project is in, and what the main problems are.

Key point: It's easy to see what should be happening.

In the Lean system, standards are linked to action. A thick volume on a shelf has little meaning. But a clear image posted at the point of use has power. Consider a quality standard for, say, paint finish. Here are three types of standards and their relative power:

- Written description in the supervisor's desk drawer: low power
- Picture posted in the workplace: higher power
- Actual sample of both good and bad conditions posted at the point of use: highest power

Hence, the concept of visual management.

VISUAL MANAGEMENT—REVERSE MAGIC

A few years ago, I was invited to speak at a conference in Las Vegas. I invited Katie and Eleanor, my now teenage daughters, to join me. We took in a number of shows, including one by David Copperfield, the great magician.

David was spectacular and during his show I had a revelation. Visual management entails *reverse magic*. David Copperfield makes the elephant disappear. We have to do the opposite and make the information elephant appear!

Visual Management

The 5S system is designed to create a visual workplace, that is, a work environment that is self-explaining, self-ordering, and self-improving.[5] In a visual workplace, the out-of-standard situation is immediately obvious and employees can easily correct it. Managing thus, on the basis of exceptions, makes excellence possible. Michel Greif in his fine book, *The Visual Factory*,[6] defines the visual management triangle (Figure 3.1).

We made a grave error when we eliminated visual controls such as wall schedules and replaced them with computers. Wall charts support the visual management triangle. They involve the team and compel action.

The computer is invaluable, but not for group communication; it lacks a public interface. This is the Achilles heel of material requirement planning (MRP) and enterprise resource planning (ERP); systems[7] are invisible and thus anesthetize the workforce. When computers offer expanded visibility (e.g., displaying data on well-lit boards, with graphic displays illustrating production flow and inventories) they will play a larger role on the manufacturing floor.

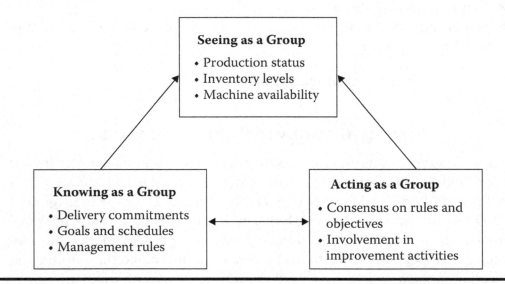

Figure 3.1   The visual management triangle.

FOUR LEVELS OF VISUAL MANAGEMENT

Lean is about making problems visible. You can't fix what you can't see. Here are the four levels of visual management in order of increasing power:

LEVEL 1—TELLS ONLY (LOWEST POWER)

Stop signs are a good example. In our neighborhood, people blow by them all the time.

I call these "Hollywood stops": the driver slows by five miles per hour, takes a perfunctory look around, and drives on through.

Visual management in many organizations gets stuck at Level 1: signage telling people what to do or not do. As Deming observed, this amounts to blaming the worker, because it subtly shifts responsibility from senior management to frontline workers. "Hey, I told them not to do it!"

LEVEL 2—SOMETHING CHANGES, WHICH GETS YOUR ATTENTION

Traffic lights are a good example of Level 2 visual management. "Hey, the light's changed to green. We can drive on."

Level 2 has more power because, done well, it wakes people up. In fact, Lean is all about wakefulness. "Hey, we have a problem here. We should do something!"

LEVEL 3—ORGANIZES BEHAVIOR

Home positions for tools and equipment are a good example of Level 3. In a surgery, home positions provide a nice visual confirmation that sponges, scalpels, and other equipment are back where they belong, and not inside the patient! In manufacturing, having a home position for, say, our torque wrench and gauges, ensures (a) tools are there when we need them, and, as important, (b) we know when they're *not* there. "Ah, Bonnie is doing her daily 2:00 p.m. torque audit."

Other good examples of Level 3 include the ribbed highway perimeters and studded lane lines. If you're on the median or straddling your lane, you get immediate feedback.

Recently, I saw a nice kaizen in the oncology department of a children's hospital. Infections are a major risk in such wards. How to encourage staff and parents to decontaminate their hands before they enter a patient's room? Move the hand decontamination unit to the point of entry. It's hard to enter without seeing and using it. Compliance rates are much improved, though I challenged the team to come up with a Level 4 device.

LEVEL 4—THE DEFECT IS IMPOSSIBLE

Lean veterans will recognize the *poka-yoke* concept (more in Chapter 6).

Step 1: Develop a deep grasp of our process and possible failure modes.
Step 2: Install gizmos and/or practices that make them impossible.

Manufacturing is full of poka-yokes, such as alarms on torque wrenches, and electronic lights and safety mats that disable the machine if a team member enters the line of fire. In healthcare, poka-yokes on gas lines make it impossible to misconnect gas lines.

As we get better at Lean, our visual management naturally progresses from Level 1 to Level 4.

Once we're good at Levels 1 and 2, we begin to think, "The same defect—again. How do we prevent it?"

Who is the best source of Levels 3 and 4 visual management?

Our frontline team members, hence the importance of total involvement (Chapter 7).

5S System

5S[8-10] is a deceptively simple system comprising the following:

- Sort
- Set in order
- Shine (and inspect)
- Standardize
- Sustain

At Toyota I came to see that a good 5S condition, in other words, a clean, well-ordered workplace that talks to you, is the foundation of improvement.

S1—Sort

If in doubt, throw it out.

Red-Tagging Rule of Thumb

The first principle of visual order is to sort out what you don't need. The workplace can get overrun with stuff: parts, work-in-process, scrap, jigs, storage shelves, bins, filing cabinets, documents, desks, chairs, racks, cabinets, phones, packaging material, tools, machinery, equipment, and so on. Some of this stuff is needed to meet your objectives, but much of it is not. Piles of stuff accumulate and impede the flow of work. Hassles increase, and long lead times become chronic.

Just-in-Case Management

Many of us are pack rats. My father, for example, has three or four ancient vacuum cleaners in his garage. His attitude is, "I'll hold on to it—just in case." (You never know when a 1963 vacuum cleaner will come in handy.) Thus, stuff accumulates. Once useful objects, now obsolete, are never discarded. A vicious cycle ensues. Their presence makes it harder to tell what is needed. We spend precious time trying to tell the difference. Moreover, these unneeded items take up more and more precious shelf and floor space. Eventually, we conclude that we need more floor space as well as more shelving, more pallets, more forklifts, and bigger warehouses, not to mention more people to operate and manage them. The clutter also creates safety hazards such as slip, trip, and fall hazards; pinch points; and blind corners.

Red Tagging

Define what you need to meet your production objectives and clear out everything else.

The key S1 tool is red tagging.

The red tag is a simple tag containing the following information:

- Item classification
- Item ID and quantity
- Reason for red tagging
- Work section
- Date

Red tags are attached to unneeded items during the sort phase of 5S. The following are the key supports for the red-tag technique.[11]

1. *Set up a red-tag removal location.* This can be a shelving unit or roped-off area of the shop floor.
2. *Schedule a red-tag pause.* This breathing period may be a few days or weeks. It gives people a chance to make recycling or disposal arrangements and gives managers and supervisors a chance to review the items before they get tossed.
3. *Explore recycling options.* Much unwanted stuff doesn't look like junk. To become a good corporate citizen during S1, recycle directly, resell, or barter, and hold a yard sale.
4. *Set up a capital assets disposal procedure.* Use a red-tag disposal form to ensure there is an audit trail for substantial capital assets.
5. *Measure red-tag volume.* To measure S1, count the number of dumpsters filled, weigh the items tossed, track the number of liberated shelves and racks, and calculate the area of floor space liberated.
6. *Commit to regular red tagging.* Hold an annual red-tag week. Some companies do red tagging once per quarter using a red-tag cart that goes around the last Friday of each quarter.

The red tag is, in effect, an order of execution. The "criminal" is taken to the red-tag removal location. Anyone can plead the case for a stay of execution. The team makes the final decision.

5S AT NEW UNITED MOTOR MANUFACTURING INC.

As noted in the last chapter, in 1983 Toyota invested in GM's failed Fremont, California, plant. More than 5,000 workers had lost their jobs and their hopes rested on a successful new model launch. But Toyota was told there was no space for a new line.

By applying 5S principles, team members liberated 30% of the floor space, more than enough for a new line. The first new Chevrolet Nova came off the line in December 1984 and NUMMI never looked back. Over the years NUMMI won multiple JD Power Gold Medals for quality.

Sadly, in 2009 a bankrupt GM pulled out of the joint venture, forcing NUMMI's closure. A valedictory piece ran in *Popular Mechanics*: "How a Plant Changed the Culture of Car Making."

But in September 2011, Tesla Motor Company announced it was purchasing the NUMMI site and would produce the Model S sedan there. Tesla President, Elon Musk, said hiring ex-NUMMI workers would be a priority and hoped to expand employment to preshutdown levels. Last I checked the Tesla plant had hired more than 1,000 team members.

S2—Set in Order

A place for everything, and everything in its place.

Proverb

Now we are ready to organize what's left so as to minimize wasted motion. How do we place our machines, tools, storage shelves, and so on, to reduce the muda of motion?

Rationalize Locations

Pick a pilot area and on two large pieces of paper, draw two maps describing:[12]

- What is
- What could be

Draw area boundaries and make up two sets of small sticky notes representing the stuff in the area (to scale).

Attach the sticky notes to the what-is map to show your current condition. Now with red string, or red stick-on arrows, show how material currently moves. In many workplaces, the result will be a spaghetti diagram. Post a large chart next to the what-is map and invite team members to write in current hassles, possible countermeasures, and comments. Leave the chart up for at least a week and invite feedback.

Now construct the what-could-be map in the same manner. Try to address the hassles identified by team members. Respond to each suggestion on the posted chart. Try to minimize wasted motion. Show material flows as you did for the what-is map. Have you reduced wasted motion? Does the new layout make sense to everyone? Again, leave the map up for at least a week and invite feedback.

The difference between the two maps will be telling. Through this process you will learn to see in a new way. You probably won't reach consensus on where every piece should go. And maybe you can't move that press cutter. Don't be discouraged. You will certainly have made large gains, and 5S is not a one-shot deal.

Now comes the reality check. In an empty part of the plant, or in the parking lot (weather permitting), draw your proposed layout with tape or chalk. Use cardboard to represent large pieces of equipment. Use colored chalk to show material movement. Does everything flow? Is there enough room to do your work? Are there any unpleasant surprises? Any additional improvements you can make? Make the corresponding changes on the what-could-be map. When you have confirmed your layout, you are ready to move equipment.

Organize and Apply Colors

Now we can organize what is left along the three dimensions and apply color to the workplace. The three keys to organizing are[13]

Where?
What?
How many?

To fix the positions of equipment and parts racks, tape out the home position on the floor. For tools and jigs, make a shadow board. To fix the positions of parts and materials, you should develop a grid system (similar to that of city streets) and give each area a simple address. Make up large visible signboards identifying the equipment, material, or process, and attach or hang them in the appropriate locations.

Show the number of units using a visual system such as a piece of colored tape showing the maximum and minimum levels, or a footprint. You should also tape out walkways, mobile equipment routes, and the perimeter of opening doors.

Develop a color standard and apply it to your workplace. You may wish to use existing ANSI standards. Your objective should be transparency. The location of everything must be so clear that

■ Anyone can find anything at any time.
■ Out-of-standard situations are obvious to everyone.

S3—Shine (and Inspect)

Nothing raises your team's spirit like a clean, well-ordered workplace. Nothing depresses the spirit more than a bleak filthy workplace. S1 and S2 will have freed up a great deal of floor and shelf space and cleaning will be much easier. Now let's apply our 5S mantra to S3. What is our standard? Our 5S team has to decide:

- What to clean
- How to clean
- Who will do the cleaning
- How clean is clean

Cleaning targets include storage areas, equipment and machinery, and surroundings (aisles, windows, meeting rooms, offices, under stairs, and so on). Develop checksheets outlining what should be cleaned. Be as specific as you can.

Cleaning methods should also be determined and appropriate supplies provided in a central area. The 5S stations should be set up and stocked with at least the following supplies: broom, dustpan, hand brush, mop and bucket, bag of wiping rags, and a large trash bin.

Cleaning responsibilities and schedules should be prominently posted. Team members should sign off on the sheets when they have completed their cleaning schedules. Make "5S-minute cleaning" a part of each job. This enhances ownership and mutual respect among your team members. We want our team members to feel that, "This is my work area and my machinery and I am going to take care of it."

S3 also means inspect. Your production team members need to regularly check the condition of their equipment. Train them so they can recognize minor changes in sound, smell, vibration, temperature, or other telltale signs. Develop inspection checksheets for machinery to support this activity.

Finally, train your team members to solve the root cause of cleanliness problems. Why are the chips there? What is causing that leak? How can we prevent these dust emissions?

S4—Standardize

Rust never sleeps.

Neil Young

We have now progressed through the first three steps of the 5S system. We should have a fine-looking workplace by now. We have

- Removed all our junk and organized what's left along three dimensions
- Given clear addresses, home positions, or both, to production and storage areas, machines, tools, jigs, and inventory
- Color-coded the workplace
- Made everything shine through 5S cleaning schedules and 5S stations
- Improved machine performance through regular cleaning and inspection

We have achieved a good condition: a clean well-ordered workplace that speaks to us.

But as Neil Young has observed, things tend to fall apart. This is the second law of thermodynamics (or Murphy's law). How are we going to maintain our good condition?

We must develop and apply standards for S1 to S3. Once we have done that, we have to develop standards for how we do our work. This is standardized work, our playbook, so to speak.

Remember that the best standards are clear, simple, and visual. Effective standards make the out-of-standard condition obvious. For example, a tool shadow board is a standard that tells us

- What tools should be here
- What tools currently are here
- Who has taken a tool and when they will return it

A production board on which kanbans[14] are posted is also a standard. It tells us

- What to make
- How many to make
- By when

It also tells us whether our production is ahead or behind. (If the production kanbans start to pile up, we are behind and everyone will know that there is a problem in our process.)

Standards for S1 to S3

- S1 (sort) standards should tell us
  - What is needed and not needed
  - Red-tag targets, frequency, and responsibilities
  - Disposal procedures
- S2 (set-in-order) standards should tell us
  - What signboards should look like and where they should be posted
  - What different colors mean
  - Where people can walk
  - Dangerous areas
  - What protective clothing is required
  - What equipment signage and footprints should look like
- S3 (shine and inspect) standards should tell us
  - What to clean and inspect
  - How to clean and inspect
  - Who cleans and when
  - Who is responsible for making sure that a given area is cleaned and inspected

We should also have a standardized approach to measuring our 5S condition. This usually means a 5S scorecard tailored to our workplace and a standard checking schedule. Measurement never fails.

Finally, we should make 5S part of our standardized work. For example, we could implement five-minute, end-of-shift 5S. Thus, employees would hand over their work area in a good condition to the next shift.

S5—Sustain

> Perseverance is all.
>
> **Theodore Roosevelt**

How do we ensure that 5S develops deep roots in our company and becomes our normal way of doing business? Involvement is the key. 5S must belong to our team members. Promotion, communication, and training are the means.

5S Promotion and Communication

Here are some 5S promotional ideas:

- *5S report boards.* Set up a central report board that shows 5S targets, current status, 5S "catch of the month," and before and after photographs.
- *5S catch of the month.* Recognize excellent 5S work. Have the president present the team member with a token of appreciation (e.g., a road safety kit or golf shirt). Post it on 5S report boards and the company intranet.
- *5S slogan or logo contests.* Involve team members in giving their activity a unique identity. At one company, team members came up with the term WOW, for War on Waste, and a corresponding graphic.
- *5S core group.* This team is responsible for sustaining 5S. Ask for a volunteer from each plant operating area. Provide any required support such as copying, word-processing, computer access, and a promotional budget.

5S Training

5S should be incorporated into your overall Lean training plan. Determine who gets what level of training; then provide it. Here is a basic training plan:

- Team member: Introduction to 5S—two hours
- 5S core group member: Implementing 5S—one day
- Supervisors and managers: Implementing 5S—one day

5S training is an investment with a quick payback. It introduces team members to the language of Lean production and lays the foundation for all future activity.

LEAN IN THE OFFICE—MAKING THE INVISIBLE, VISIBLE

Imagine watching a baseball or football game without a scoreboard. Pretty boring, no?

Now imagine walking through a typical design, engineering, sales, law, or human resources office.

What do we see? People, computers, cubicles.

Can we tell if we're winning or losing? Are we meeting customer needs? What are our targets? What are our biggest problems? What countermeasures are in place, and are they working?

In most offices it's hard to know. Office work is invisible, unlike manufacturing work. We can't see the flow of design projects, for example, the way we can see cars flow in an auto plant. Peter Drucker called such work "knowledge" work. Most knowledge work is hidden in the box known as a computer. Our job is to get it out of the box and up on the wall, where everyone can see it.

How do we make office work visible? Let's stick with design, with the understanding that these ideas can be broadly applied:

■ To illustrate the flow of work, develop a visual tool that mirrors your process (e.g., a pipeline). Hold regular team huddles there, wherein project leaders provide status summaries.
■ Use cards to show projects assigned per team member. Stacking cards allows you to see each team member's workload. Unassigned projects or tasks can go into a visible queue.
■ Track progress with simple visuals including Red/Green dots, hand-drawn Gant charts, or a simple timeline with five or six key milestones.
■ Keep a simple scorecard around customer needs: Met/Not Met, On Time/Not on Time, On Budget/Not on Budget.
■ Make the top five problems and countermeasure status visible. Your visible action log should include three Cs—Concern, Cause, Countermeasure—and two Ws—Who and When.
■ Keep things binary (OK/Not OK) to force problems to the surface.

Initially, some people may object and say, "Why do all this? It's all in the computer." But the computer doesn't satisfy the visual management triangle. Moreover, the computer is often wrong!

Total Productive Maintenance

The performance standard is zero breakdowns.

Seiichi Nakajima

5S naturally leads to total productive maintenance (TPM), which is the key to machine stability and effectiveness.[15] As you progress in your Lean production journey, you will inevitably wish to train your team members so they

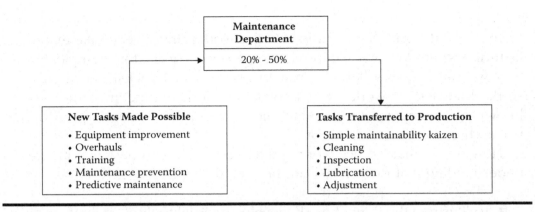

Figure 3.2   How TPM shifts maintenance tasks.

can look after their equipment. TPM assigns basic maintenance work such as inspection, cleaning, lubricating, and tightening to production team members. This frees up maintenance team members for predictive maintenance, equipment improvement and overhauls, training, and other high-value activities, as illustrated in Figure 3.2.[16]

TPM represents a profound shift from the "I operate; you fix" mindset, to "We are all responsible for our equipment, our plant, and our future." Just as in safety, where the target is zero accidents, the target of TPM is zero breakdowns.

> **MAINTENANCE STAGES**
>
> Stage 1: Breakdown maintenance (firefighting)
> Stage 2: Preventive maintenance (some proactive planning and troubleshooting)
> Stage 3: TPM = (Preventive + Predictive maintenance) + Total involvement

Key Measures

The key measures of machine effectiveness are[17,18]

- *Availability. Availability* = (loading time − downtime)/loading time; a measure of uptime.
- *Performance efficiency.* Performance efficiency = (net operating time − lost time)/(net operating time); a measure of efficiency while the machine is running.
- *Overall equipment effectiveness (OEE).* OEE = availability × performance efficiency × quality rate; a measure of overall equipment efficiency.

Accurate data is essential. But some managers feel that time spent by workers measuring machine performance is time wasted. Some companies do not even record equipment failure downtime unless it exceeds 30 minutes. A minority measures speed losses.

At Toyota I learned that focus is everything in maintenance. Thus, we need accurate equipment operation records, and not just of downtime. Fortunately, technological advances have made this data much more accessible. For a relatively small investment, most companies can readily generate mean time to repair (MTTR), mean time between failure (MTBF), and other useful data for their critical equipment.

Once we have identified our hot spots, we can back them up with manual processes or additional buffers. This in turn gives us the time we need to solve the root causes of our equipment problems. Only thus can we escape the endless firefighting that afflicts most maintenance efforts.

Six Big Losses

TPM entails involving all team members to eliminate the six big losses that downgrade machine effectiveness:[19]

Downtime

1. Equipment breakdowns
2. Setup and adjustment delays (e.g., because of die changes in stamping presses or injection molding machines)

Speed or Hidden Losses

3. Idling and minor stoppages (the machine is being run but no product is processed)
4. Reduced speed (the actual machine speed is less than the design speed)

Defects

5. Process defects (e.g., scrap, defects that require repair)
6. Reduced yield (e.g., from machine startup to stable production)

Many companies do not track OEE. They would be shocked if they did. The average company has an OEE of less than 50%. In other words, equipment is being used at less than half its effectiveness.

How can this be? Well, most companies have a reasonable idea of their machine availability. Breakdowns are dramatic events that get everyone's attention, but minor stoppages are rarely tracked. And the minor or hidden failures that cause no immediate function loss are almost never tracked.

Speed or Hidden Losses

These are the most difficult to track. For example, a machine's motor is running, but no product is being processed because

- There is a jam and no product is coming into the machine.
- A machine downstream is down ("blocked").
- We are out of parts ("starved").
- The machine is out of adjustment and must be readjusted.
- A sensor is misaligned and must be reset.

Another example is a machine running at a reduced speed because of

- Worn out or dirty equipment
- Insufficient debugging during startup

Accordingly, we should organize our maintenance activities around the life cycle of the equipment, which typically follows the so-called bathtub curve shown in Figure 3.3.[20]

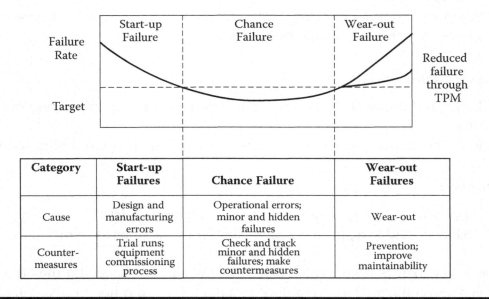

Category	Start-up Failures	Chance Failure	Wear-out Failures
Cause	Design and manufacturing errors	Operational errors; minor and hidden failures	Wear-out
Counter-measures	Trial runs; equipment commissioning process	Check and track minor and hidden failures; make countermeasures	Prevention; improve maintainability

Figure 3.3   Lifespan characteristics and maintenance activities.

BASIC IMAGE OF TPM—MOTHER AND CHILD

Consider a mother with a young baby. She monitors the child's health and is able to take care of most of the child's needs. If the baby's temperature rises a little, the mother gives the child medicine. If the baby has diaper rash, she applies zinc oxide ointment.

If the fever persists, however, she will call the doctor. As well, she will schedule regular checkups to ensure the child is well.

Like a mother, the production worker monitors the machine's condition and can handle most of its needs. These include simple cleaning, inspection, lubrication, tightening, and adjustment. The production worker will call the doctor (maintenance) when an upset condition persists or for routine checkups.

The Machine Loss Pyramid

To understand machine losses better, let us borrow a concept from safety management. Herbert Heinrich, in his landmark 1931 text, *Industrial Accident Prevention*, proposed that for every serious injury, there were 10 minor injuries, 30 property damage incidents (but no personal injury), and 600 near misses. A similar concept applies to machine losses (Figure 3.4). The absolute numbers are less important than the concept.

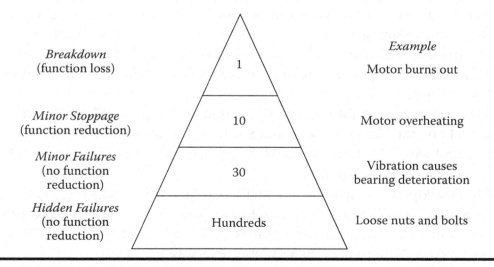

Figure 3.4   The machine loss pyramid.

Let us define our terms:

- Breakdown means function loss.
- Minor stoppage means function reduction.
- Minor failure means a substandard condition or incident that does cause function loss (e.g., elevated temperature or pressure, vibration, scratches, dust, and chip emissions).
- Hidden failure means a condition that may lead to a minor failure (e.g., loose nuts and bolts, lubricant breakdown, warping, or stretching).

What does the figure tell us?

1. Breakdown (function loss) incidents are merely the tip of the iceberg.
2. Minor stoppages (function deterioration) may be more important than breakdowns.
3. There are probably hundreds of minor and hidden failures for every machine breakdown.
4. To prevent breakdowns, we must track and prevent these hundreds of minor and hidden failures.

The early signs that may foreshadow an accident, which I have called hidden and minor failures, are called *warusa-kagen* in Japanese. These are anomalies that do not cause any function loss but whose detection helps prevent breakdowns and improves our understanding of our equipment.

Minor anomalies often fail to attract our attention. When driving a car, for example, we might ignore a strange noise in the car's motor, as long as the car is running well. We might wait for the breakdown before responding. TPM means listening and watching for anomalies and taking action before the breakdown.

Masaaki Imai describes a production unit at the Tokai Rika plant in Japan where machinists are encouraged to report all warusa-kagen or "quasi-problems."[21] These are tracked, and team members with especially good eyes receive recognition.

We developed a similar activity at Toyota Cambridge, which we called Take Action on Accident Prevention. Its overwhelming success helped propel the plant to industry leadership in safety and machine effectiveness. We typically received thousands of Take Actions every year.

How do we use these insights to support our TPM activities?

Small-Group Activity

We need to involve production team members in checking, reporting, and, where possible, correcting hidden failures and minor stoppages. We need to develop checksheets for each major piece of equipment and a system to track and make visible our condition.

Figure 3.5 shows a generic TPM checksheet. Ideally, production and maintenance team members develop these jointly. Figure 3.6 shows a TPM checksheet that might be used in a repair area.

Once we have identified our hot spots we can strengthen them by involving our team members in kaizen circles, practical kaizen training, and other small group activity. Thus, we

- Strengthen OEE and extend the lifespan of our machines
- Strengthen the capability of our team members and processes
- Increase respect for humanity

Figure 3.7 summarizes the stages of TPM. Our long-term Lean implementation strategy should incorporate this image.

Summary

5S and TPM are two keys to achieving production stability. 5S is a system of workplace organization and standardization whose goal is to support visual management. Visual management means managing by exceptions. In

Department _____ Section _____	
Month _____ Team _____	
Machine _____ Machine No. _____	
Key Checkpoints_____	
Standards_____	
Day: 1 2 3 4 5 6 7 8 9 10 11 12 13 14 15 16 17 18 19 20 21 22	
Result 1	
Result 2	
Result 3	
Comments	

Figure 3.5 Sample TPM checksheet.

Power Tools	Tool No.	1	2	3	4	5	6	8	9	10	12	13	14	15	17	18
TPM Check		Skill Saw	Jig Saw	Small Drill	Large Drill	Small Die Grinder	Large Die Grinder	Palm Sander	Disk Grinder	In-Line Gun	Glue Gun	Chop Saw	Mitre Saw	Welder	Drill Press	Table Saw
No.	Detail	E	E	E	E	P	P	P	P	E	E	E	E	E	E	E
1	*Cleanliness*															
1-1	Tool is free of dirt / grease/ or oil															
1-2	All moving / rotating parts can be easily inspected															
2	*Mechanical*															
2-1	Signs of wear or fatigue															
2-2	Cracked or damaged casings															
2-3	All guards in place and in good condition (if applicable)															
2-4	Chuck or arbour condition															
2-5	Arbour 'keeper' bolt / nut in good condition															
2-6	Tool lubrication (per spec).															
2-7	Excessive vibration															
3	*Electrical*															
3-1	Electrical cord and plug condition															
3-2	Trigger & lock operation															
3-3	Ground pin condition (if applicable)															
3-4	Excessive arcing and/or rough operation															
3-5	Excessive vibration															
3-6	Wear or general damage to casing															
4	*General*															
4-1	All set screws & locking screws set to manufacturer's specs?															
4-2	Did previous user leave in good condition?															

Monthly Safety Tip	Legend		Tool Type	Team Member: _____
		Good Condition	**Electric**	Team Leader: _____
				_____ / 2001
		Unacceptable (remove)	**Pneumatic**	
Ensure that all set screws are flush or below the surface of any rotating parts. The position of this set screw on this sander caused an injury	Key	If the tool is designated as unacceptable please take it out of service & repair or replace		

Figure 3.6   Sample TPM checksheet for repair area.

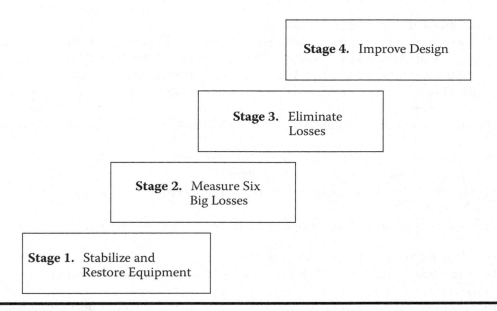

Figure 3.7   TPM stages.

a visual workplace out-of-standard conditions are immediately obvious and can be quickly corrected.

5S naturally leads to TPM, through which production team members become involved in basic maintenance activities. TPM targets the six big losses that afflict equipment. The Machine Loss Pyramid concept highlights the importance of the identifying hidden and minor losses early on. By involving our production team members in checking and improving equipment performance we harvest substantial benefits.

Endnotes

1. Toyota training document.
2. We do not address material stability here. Lean companies confirm parts and raw materials using the well-developed techniques of quality management. Toyota goes one step further and actively supports suppliers through its Operations Management Consulting Division, and in North America, its Toyota Suppliers Support Center.
3. For example, US federal environmental standards now comprise 17 volumes and 35,000 pages. Who can possibly keep track of, let alone understand, such standards? Phillip Howard has argued that when the law (i.e., standards) loses touch with common sense, we have no internal compass to guide our behavior (*The Death of Common Sense: How Law Is Suffocating America* [New York: Warner Books, 1996]).

4. Discussion with Toyota executive.
5. Gwendolyn Galsworth, *Visual Systems* (New York: AMACOM, 1997).
6. Michel Greif, *The Visual Factory* (Portland, OR: Productivity Press, 1991).
7. Over the past decade or so MRP and ERP software has been used to schedule production, determine parts requirements and delivery times, and so on. More in Chapter 5.
8. Hiroyuki Hirano, *5 Pillars of the Visual Workplace* (Portland, OR: Productivity Press, 1995).
9. Toyota Motor Corporation, Operations Management Consulting Division, *The Toyota Production System* (Tokyo, 1995).
10. The corresponding Japanese words are *seiri*, *seiton*, *seiso*, *seiketsu*, and *shitsuke*.
11. Gwendolyn Galsworth, *Visual Systems* (New York: AMACOM, 1997).
12. Ibid.
13. Hiroyuki Hirano, *Putting 5S to Work* (Tokyo: PHP Institute, 1993).
14. A *kanban*, usually a card, is an authorization to produce or withdraw a part or product.
15. Seiichi Nakajima, *Total Productive Maintenance* (Portland, OR: Productivity Press, 1988).
16. Ibid.
17. Ibid.
18. Edward Hartmann, *Successfully Installing TPM in a Non-Japanese Plant* (Pittsburgh: TPM Press, 1992).
19. Ibid. Hartmann also recommends measuring total effective equipment productivity (TEEP), which is the product of OEE and equipment utilization.
20. Seiichi Nakajima, *Total Productive Maintenance* (Portland, OR: Productivity Press, 1988).
21. Masaaki Imai, *Kaizen: The Key to Japan's Competitive Success* (New York: McGraw-Hill, 1986).

Study Questions

1. What is a standard? What are the attributes of an effective standard?
2. Define the visual management triangle. Can you describe a workplace where you have seen it applied effectively? What are the key enablers?
3. Take a walk in your workplace.
    a. See if you can find at least one example of Levels 1, 2, 3, and 4 visual management.
    b. What are the most common visual management levels used in your workplace? Any reflections or learning points?
    c. How might you improve visual management in your workplace?
4. Take another walk in your workplace.
    a. Assess each element of 5S.
    b. Any reflections or learning points?
    c. How might you improve 5S in your workplace?
5. Define the most important measures of machine performance.
6. Identify at least one example of each of the Six Big Losses in your workplace.
    a. What are possible causes of each type of loss?
    b. How might you improve machine stability and effectiveness in your workplace?
7. Do the principles of total productive maintenance apply outside the factory? Explain your answer with concrete examples.

Chapter 4

Standardized Work

Improvement is endless and eternal.

Toyota Proverb

Standardized work is our playbook: the safest, easiest, and most effective way of doing the job that we currently know. At Toyota I came to understand that

- There is no one best way to do the work.
- Workers should design the work.
- The purpose of standardized work is to provide a basis for improvement.

Even our best processes are rife with muda. Therefore, standardized work constantly changes.

Sadly, in many organizations standardization becomes a straitjacket, another instrument of command and control management. "Thou shalt do as I say," thunders the senior manager, effectively crippling improvement efforts. We need to deepen our understanding of standardization.

Methods Engineering versus Lean Thinking

Fred Taylor introduced the "single best way" concept a century ago. Frank and Lillian Gilbreth refined the concept and developed the tools of methods engineering that industrial engineers still use. Industrial engineering practice is based on the following unwritten assumptions:[1]

1. There is a single best way (and the engineers will find it).
2. Workers are not involved in designing the work or making improvements.
3. Standards rarely change (and only the experts can change them).[2]

These ideas were important breakthroughs a century ago but have outlived their usefulness.

What Do We Have to Manage?

Let us take a systems view (Figure 4.1). Our goal is to provide a required level of output (goods or services) that meets our expectations and those of our customer for PQCDSM:

■ Productivity
■ Quality
■ Cost
■ Delivery time
■ Safety and environment
■ Morale

Our tools are the 4 Ms:

■ Man/woman: our team members
■ Machine: our equipment, jigs, conveyors, and so on
■ Material: the raw materials and parts our suppliers provide
■ Method: our processes

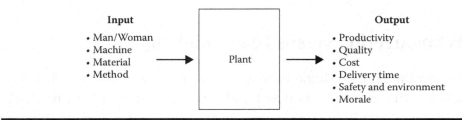

Input

• Man/Woman
• Machine
• Material
• Method

Plant

Output

• Productivity
• Quality
• Cost
• Delivery time
• Safety and environment
• Morale

Figure 4.1   A systems view.

Method is the mix of man/woman, machine, and material. Standardized work is a tool for developing, confirming, and improving our method (processes). A process is simply a set of steps or actions with a clearly defined goal.[3] The process tells the team member what to do, when to do it, and in what order.

Maximize Utilization of Machines or People?

Many of us have been taught that to improve efficiency we must improve machine utilization. We must reconsider. To maximize machine utilization we must

- Run machines constantly and as fast as possible, which creates overproduction muda.
- Retain extra people to keep the machines running.
- Increase work-in-process to cover problems and keep the machines running.

In other words, we must engage in wasteful activities.

By contrast, Toyota seeks to maximize the utilization of people.[4] Human flexibility provides benefits that dwarf those provided by machine utilization. For example, an operator can

- Move from machine to machine to make items as they are required.
- Load machines and transfer parts easily, whereas machine cost increases exponentially with automatic loading and transferring.
- Easily adjust work cycles in response to demand changes.

The corollary is that small simple machines are generally preferable to big complex ones ("monuments") because they are

- Cheaper (and can often be manufactured in-house)
- More robust (fewer moving parts)
- Adjust to demand changes easily (e.g., if demand doubles, we can add another small machine. If demand is halved, we can idle the machine half the time at low cost.)

Labor Density

Thus, in the Lean system standardized work is focused on human movement. We seek to develop people-centered processes that flow smoothly and safely. Our measure of efficiency is labor density defined as follows:[5]

$$Labor\ density = Work/Motion$$

Customer demand determines the numerator. Toyota's approach is to continually reduce the denominator.

LEAN IN A KINDERGARTEN CLASS

My wife, Pamela, teaches kindergarten, and Lean fundamentals are a big part of it. Her classroom is full of excellent 5S, visual management, and standardized work. There's a place for everything, and not surprisingly, everything is in its place. Kids thrive in Pam's class because they're relaxed. Kids, she says, need structure more than anything (except love). Lean fundamentals also free Pam up so she can focus on the kids, as opposed to looking for stuff, or dealing with other avoidable hassles.

My dear wife even teaches the scientific method in a way that Lean learners would recognize. Her science module begins, "What do scientists do?":

1. I make a hypothesis.
2. I observe what actually happens.
3. And then I adjust my hypothesis!

Why do we continually neglect the basics?

Why Standardized Work?

Standardized work provides great benefits:[6]

1. *Process stability:* Stability means repeatability. We need to meet our productivity, quality, cost, lead time, safety, and environmental targets every time.
2. *Clear stop and start points for each process:* These and knowledge of our takt, that is, our pace of production rationalized with our rate of

sales and cycle times, allow us to see our production condition at a glance. Are we ahead or behind? Is there a problem?

3. *Organizational learning:* Standardized work preserves know-how and expertise. If a veteran employee leaves, we won't lose his or her experience.

4. *Audit and problem solving:* Standardized work allows us to assess our current condition and identify problems. Checkpoints and vital process steps are easy to track. We are able to ask important questions:
   a. Are team members able to do the process smoothly or are they falling behind?
   b. If they are falling behind, by how much and in what job elements?
   c. How can we improve these elements?

5. *Employee involvement and poka-yoke:* In the Lean system team members develop standardized work, supported by supervisors and engineers. Moreover, team members identify opportunities for simple, inexpensive error-proofing or poka-yoke devices.

6. *Kaizen:* Our processes are mainly muda. Once we have achieved process stability, we are ready to improve. Standardized work provides the baseline against which we measure improvement

7. *Training:* Standardized work provides a basis for employee training.
   a. Once operators are familiar with standardized work formats, it becomes second nature for them to do the job according to standards. Vital steps and checkpoints serve as constant reminders. Because process training is easier, we can more easily respond to changes in demand (and the corresponding changes in takt time and process steps).

Prerequisites for Standardized Work

We cannot work to standards when there are continuous line stoppages and slowdowns. Here are common sources of instability:

- Quality problems with incoming parts
- Problems with machinery, jigs, or tools
- Parts shortages
- A less than full condition (which means that the team member may have to wait for a part to work on)[7]
- Safety problems such as poor ergonomic layouts; slip, trip, and falling hazards; exposed pinch points; and so on

Lean activities support stability. Machine stability requires 5S and TPM. Quality is strengthened with jidoka. Just-in-time techniques attack parts shortage problems. 5S, TPM, and standardized work improve safety.

THE GREAT PARADOX

My Toyota senseis taught me to develop simple visual standards for all important things. Standardized work, they explained, comprises:

- Work content
- Sequence
- Timing
- Expected outcome
- Embedded tests that signal OK/Not OK (more in Chapter 6)

Exacting and restricting, no?

Let me tell you a story. My wife's kindergarten class is full of kids with special needs. Some are not expected to speak or read with any proficiency. Basic activities such as tying shoe laces, washing hands, and going to the bathroom, are difficult and rife with anxiety for them.

So Pam developed simple visual standardized work for basic tasks. Here's but one example:

How does this help the kids?

For a start, their anxiety level goes way down, and confidence goes up! They can relax and focus on learning. One little fellow, who I'll call Carlos, was not expected to ever speak coherently, or to read. His parents insisted he stay in Pam's class for two years—for the learning—and

supplemented his development with occupational therapy at home. Two years later Carlos is a very chatty, confident little reader.
  Standardized work sets you free.

Elements of Standardized Work

Standardized work comprises three elements:[8-10]

- Takt time.
- Work sequence—What is the best way to do the process?
- In-process stock—How much inventory should there be?

These provide a baseline against which we can assess a given process.[11]

Takt Time

Takt time tells us our demand frequency, or how frequently we must produce a product, and can be calculated as follows:

$$Takt = Daily\ operating\ time \div Required\ quantity\ per\ day^{12}$$

For example, if our daily order is 890 units and we operate two 445-minute shifts, our takt time would be:

$$Takt = 890 \div (445 + 445)\ units = 1\ minute$$

We would have to produce one product every minute.

Takt Time and Cycle Time

Takt time differs from *cycle time*, which is the actual time it takes to do the process. Our goal is to synchronize takt time and cycle time to the greatest extent possible. This allows us to integrate processes into cells in support of our goal of one-at-a-time production.
  A cell is an arrangement of people, machines, materials, and methods such that processing steps are adjacent in sequential order so that parts can be processed one at a time (or in some cases in a consistent small batch that is

maintained through the process sequence). The purpose of a cell is to achieve and maintain efficient continuous flow (which is discussed in Chapter 5).

Takt time also allows us to grasp our production condition at a glance. For example, if takt time is 1 minute, we should see a product moving past us every minute.[13] If a product moved past every two minutes, we would know that there was a problem downstream. This shared understanding motivates quick countermeasures, to get the line moving again, and a kaizen, to eliminate the root cause of the problem.

Work Sequence

The work sequence defines the order in which the work is done in a given process. For example, the team member might have to

- Pick up the part
- Walk to the machine
- Place the part in the machine and process the part
- Take the part to the next machine

We have to clearly define the best way to do each job action and the proper sequence. At Toyota, where possible, we used pictures and drawings to show

- Proper posture
- How the hands and feet should move
- How to hold the tools
- Accumulated know-how or the ins and outs of the job
- Critical quality or safety item

I found that our team members had confidence in standardized work developed in this way.[14]

At Toyota, the people-focus and visual nature of standardized work make it a powerful tool for safety and ergonomics.[15] A clear picture of the proper posture or hand position, for example, is a constant reminder as well as a subtle challenge to eliminate awkward postures and other ergonomic risk factors.

In-Process Stock

In-process stock is the minimum number of unfinished work pieces required for the operator to complete the process without standing in front of a machine. The determining factor is that work cannot progress without a certain number of pieces on hand.

We must increase in-process stock in the following circumstances:

- Quality checks require additional work pieces.
- Temperatures must fall before the next operation can commence.
- Machinery cycles automatically.
- Machine operation is in reverse order of the processes.

Defining in-process stock establishes work-in-process (WIP) standards per process and, again, makes abnormalities obvious.

IS STANDARDIZED WORK DEHUMANIZING?

In my experience standardized work supports human creativity, provided the team leader has the right understanding. Standardized work is a process, not a prison. Our goal is perfection, a process with zero waste. Standardized work provides the foundation, team member involvement the impetus for endless and eternal improvement.

Charts Used to Define Standardized Work

Our team members develop standardized work supported by engineers and other experts as required. Three charts are used:[16,17]

- Production capacity chart
- Standardized work combination table
- Standardized work analysis chart

Each is a tool for analyzing and defining a process and for identifying improvement points.

Production Capacity Chart

This chart determines the capacity of the machines in a process. It documents machine and manual times and allows us to identify bottlenecks at a glance. Production capacity for a given machine is calculated using the following formula:

Capacity = Operational time per shift ÷ (Process time + Setup time/interval)

Setup time refers to the time required to change from one machine setting to another. Setup for a punch press might include changing the die, adjusting the machine settings, and loading a new coil of steel. The interval refers to the frequency of setup in terms of number of parts.

Figure 4.2[18] shows an actual chart. The production capacity of the drilling machine used in process 2 may be calculated as follows:

- Operational time = 460 minutes per shift (27,600 seconds)
- Process time = 24 seconds per part
- Time needed to replace grinding wheel = 30 seconds
- Interval = every 1,000 parts

Solution: Capacity = 27,600 seconds ÷ (24 + 30/1000) = 1,148.5 parts

The capacity of the drilling machine is 1,148 parts per shift.

Standardized Work Combination Table

This chart shows

- Work elements and their sequence
- Time per work element

Manager	Foreman	Standardized Production Capacity Sheet	Part No.	17111-38010	Unit Type	22R	Section 532 542	Name Suziki Sato	
			Part Name	Intake Manifold	No. of Units	1			
Process No.	Process Name	M/C No.	Basic Operation Time			Tool Changes		Capacity	Comments
			Manual Time	Auto Time	Time to Complete	Interval Between Changes	Time Taken		
1	Machining of Attaching Face	MIL 1764	Min Sec 3	Min Sec 25	Min Sec 28	100	1'00'''	965	
2	Drilling Bolt Hole	DR 2424	3	21	24	1000	30"	1148	
3	Tapping of Threads	TP 1101	3	11	14	1000	30"	'967	
4	Quality Check (Thread Pitch)		5		5			5520	
		Total	14						

Figure 4.2 Production capacity chart.

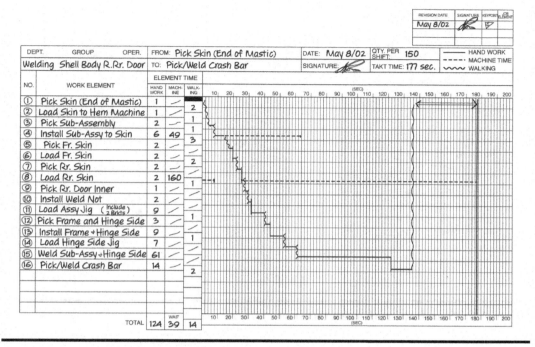

Figure 4.3 Standardized work combination table.

■ Operator and machine time
■ The interaction between operators and machines or between different operators

The chart makes kaizen easier by breaking down the movements of the operator and relating them to machine time. Figure 4.3[19] shows an actual chart.

Standardized Work Analysis Chart

This chart helps to rationalize layout and to train workers. It comprises

■ Work layout
■ Process steps and times
■ Critical quality and safety items
■ Standardized WIP stock

Figure 4.4[20] shows an actual chart.

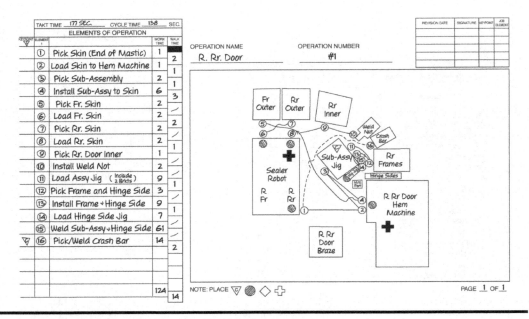

Figure 4.4   Standard work analysis chart.

Job Element Sheets

A job element is the minimum action or group of actions required to advance a process.[21] For example, picking up a bolt is an action but does not advance the process. Picking up a bolt and installing it on a work piece is a group of actions, which advances the process. Job element sheets (JES) are one-pagers that define

- ■ Actions making up the job element
- ■ Rationale
- ■ Pictures and photos highlighting key points
- ■ Revision record

Figure 4.5[22] shows an actual JES.

I have found the JES to be invaluable for recording the ins and outs of the job, the learning points gathered over years by team members. The JES is a useful intermediate step on the journey to standardized work.

Time Measurement

Time measurement entails breaking a process into its elements and measuring the instant each element starts and stops. Here are the required steps:

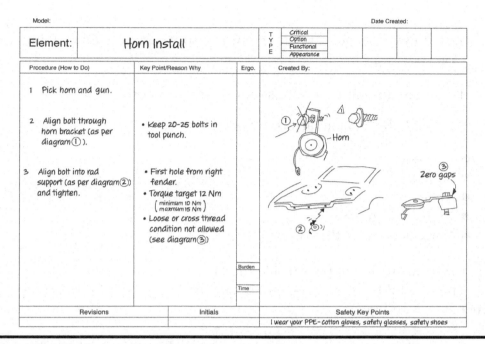

Figure 4.5 Job element sheet (JES).

1. Become familiar with the process area and its surroundings.
2. Draw the process area layout.
3. Show the work sequence.
4. Write the work elements.
5. Measure total cycle time (at least 10 times).
6. Measure the time for each work element (at least 10 times).
7. Identify and measure irregular work (e.g., clearing blockages).
8. Write the standardized work analysis chart and standardized work combination table.

At Toyota I learned that simple time measurement can reveal much about the current condition of a workplace. Are we ahead? Are we behind? How repeatable is our process? Do we have too many machines? How much value-added work is in our process?

STANDARDIZED WORK FOR KNOWLEDGE WORKERS?

What's the best way we know, right now?
How do we summarize it in one simple, visual page?

How do we engage our team members so we can continually improve our best way?

These are among Lean's most important questions.

As noted above, standardized work comprises:

- Content
- Sequence
- Time
- Expected outcome
- Embedded tests that signal OK/Not OK

Does this recipe apply outside the factory?

The embedded tests concept applies universally. As for the other elements: yes and no.

Yes: In short cycle time, repetitive knowledge work (e.g., a pharmacy filling high-volume prescriptions, or a laboratory analyzing high volumes of a given sample, or repetitive, high-volume legal work)

No: In long cycle time, nonrepetitive knowledge work (e.g., a complex, long-cycle time surgery, engineering or design process)

Standardized work and other Lean fundamentals confer great benefits outside the factory, if translated and applied with finesse. Checklists are a good example of such translation. In effect, a good checklist is a list of embedded tests. Atul Gawande's fine book, *The Checklist Manifesto*, illustrates their power in the hospital environment. By contrast, if we insisted on the above manufacturing definition in a surgery, we'd likely come to grief. Also see *The Remedy: Bringing Lean out of the Factory to Transform the Entire Organization*. (P. Dennis, New York: Wiley, 2010)

Manpower Reduction

The tools of standardized work help us improve efficiency by identifying value and waste in a process. Efficiency may be defined as follows:

$$\text{Efficiency} = \text{Output/Manpower}$$

At Toyota I learned that because output is fixed by the customer, the only way for us to improve efficiency was to reduce manpower. Workers released thereby were reassigned.

Fluctuation: Process problems that cause instability

Changeover: Product-related; changing from one product or part to another

Periodic Work: Process-related (e.g., material or tool change or cleaning weld tip)

Element Time: Value-added work, muda, incidental work (changeable and not changeable)

Figure 4.6[23] shows a useful tool called an operator balance chart for a process before and after improvement. Improvements are based on a deep understanding of what is actually happening in each process. The kaizen activity for this process has reduced its cycle time from 134 to 82 seconds. Figures 4.7[24] and 4.8[25] show before and after operator balance charts for the team.

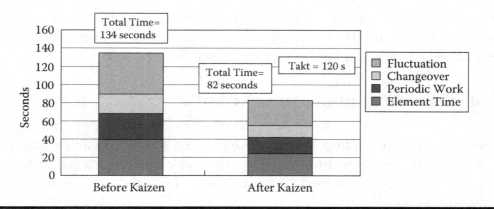

Figure 4.6   Operator balance chart.

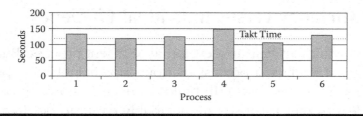

Figure 4.7   Balance chart for production line—current.

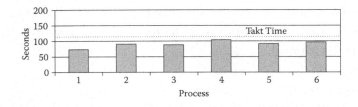

Figure 4.8 Balance chart for production line—improved.

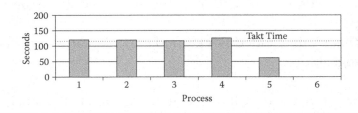

Figure 4.9 Rebalanced production.

Figure 4.9 shows how we might redistribute work to reduce manpower. As you can see, we have eliminated process 6. Note that processes 1 to 5 are "full" in the sense that cycle times equal takt time. Process 5, by contrast, constitutes about 50% of our takt time. We will seek further kaizen to eliminate this process. In the interim, by rebalancing in this manner we make visible the muda of waiting and motivate kaizen. Figure 4.10[26] provides guidelines for determining how many operators we need.

> **MANPOWER REDUCTION AT TOYOTA**
>
> At Toyota I found that workers whose processes disappeared due to rebalancing were often reassigned to kaizen teams. These assignments were prized because they were a welcome change from production, a good way to get promoted, and fun. Thus, manpower reduction came to be viewed positively.

Overall Efficiency versus Individual Efficiency

Standardized work can help us develop an efficient process. But our goal is overall efficiency. In fact, a process that outstrips neighboring processes creates inventory muda because WIP builds in front of slower processes.

Nonetheless, some processes are invariably easier to do than others. How do we promote cooperation between processes within a production area?

Remainder in # operators required calculation	Guideline/Target
< .3	Do not add extra operator. Further reduce waste and incidental work.
.3-.5	Do not add extra operator yet. After two weeks of operation and kaizen, reevaluate whether enough waste and incidental work can be removed.
> .5	Add an extra operator if necessary and keep reducing waste and incidental work to eventually eliminate the need for that operator

Figure 4.10 Guidelines for determining the number of operators in a cell.

The answer is to design standardized work for a production area such that

■ Cycle times are as balanced as possible.
■ Areas of responsibility overlap.
■ Distances between workers are as short as possible.

Organizing work in this manner improves throughput. A typical manufacturing plant comprises dependent processes in series, each subject to statistical fluctuations. In *The Goal* Eli Goldratt vividly illustrates the challenges such a system faces:[27]

■ Variables (e.g., inventory) down the line will fluctuate around the maximum deviation established by upstream processes.
■ Throughput is governed by the slowest machine in the chain (the bottleneck).

RELAY RACE METAPHOR

Taiichi Ohno emphasized that machines must not be placed around team members (like cages in a zoo). It should be easy for team members to communicate and help each other. Ohno likened this sort of teamwork to a relay race on land, where the faster runner can support the slower runner in the baton zone. Such cooperation enhances efficiency and *esprit de corps*.

Hence, Goldratt argues, we must:

1. Identify our bottlenecks.
2. Decide how to exploit the bottlenecks.
3. Elevate the bottlenecks.

Arranging processes such that team members can help each other automatically alleviates our bottlenecks.

Standardized Work and Kaizen

Standardized work is a process whose goal is kaizen. If standardized work doesn't change, we are regressing. The leader's responsibility is to maintain a good condition and to improve. Sometimes kaizen opportunities are obvious. These include obvious muda such as recurring defects, machine breakdowns, or excessive WIP. Hard-to-do work (muri) or unevenness (mura) are other obvious targets. The following sections describe design guidelines that can help us find kaizen opportunities.[28,29]

Guidelines for Economy of Motion

- Hand movements should be symmetrical and concurrent.
- Two-handed motions should be as compact as possible.
- Light work should be done with the hands and forearms, rather than the upper arms and shoulders.
- Motion should flow freely.
- Work should be done in the "strong circle" a yard in diameter and directly in front of the worker. Maintain appropriate body posture.
- Keep hands free as much as possible.

Guidelines for Layout and Equipment

- Identify home positions for tools and materials.
- Build flexibility into the layout to accommodate demand changes and taller or shorter operators.
- Move parts horizontally. Avoid vertical part movement.
- Use gravity to move parts (e.g., with sloping parts racks).
- Place tools and materials conveniently.

- Ensure adequate lighting.
- Use colors.
- Use U-shaped layouts so that process start and end points are side by side.

Guidelines for Tools and Jigs

- Develop jigs to eliminate manual holding of materials.
- Use ergonomic tools (i.e., tools that are easy to grip, encourage good hand/wrist posture, and minimize forces and vibration).
- Combine tools where possible (e.g., use a T-wrench instead of a socket wrench and screwdriver).
- Where possible, use balancers that automatically withdraw the tool from point of use.

STANDARDIZED WORK AND RESPECT FOR PEOPLE

Why should people have to work in wasteful, unsafe tasks, disconnected from purpose? Why should they go home each day frustrated, depressed, or alienated? Why not engage them in designing and improving our work? Who knows the work better than the people who do it every day?

These are self-evident truths, are they not? Through standardized work we express respect for our team members' time, effort and humanity. Knowledge waste exists at epidemic levels, especially among knowledge workers! Healthcare workers, for example, are among the best educated in all of industry. Are they engaged in developing and improving hospital work? What about people working in areas like sales, marketing, finance, human resources, and purchasing?

Standardized work expresses our team members' current best thinking. Problems become visible quicker. Training new team members is easier. Safety, quality, delivery, and cost improve. And perhaps most important, people feel good, grow, and want to do more.

Common Layouts

We typically encounter four layouts:[30,31]

- Islands (isolated processes)
- Connected islands

- Connected islands with full-work control
- Cells

Islands

Island processes are isolated from one another. Forklifts move piles of inventory between islands. Often workers in each island build as fast as they can regardless of actual demand.

Connected Islands

Conveyors or chutes connect islands. There is no mechanism to control the amount of inventory on conveyors. Workers typically build as fast as they can.

Connected Islands with Full-Work Control

Conveyors or chutes connect islands. A visual device controls the amount of inventory between processes. The upstream process stops producing when the downstream process is full.

Cells

Machines are side by side. There is minimal inventory between machines. Ideally, one piece is made at a time. As soon as a piece is processed, it moves to the next process. Figure 4.11 illustrates the four situations. Figure 4.12 summarizes the relative merit of each layout.[32]

Summary

Standardized work is a process whose goal is to identify muda so that we can continually improve through team member involvement. Lean production and methods engineering differ substantially in their approach to standardized work. I have described the elements of standardized work and the various associated charts. Through standardized work we can improve labor density by increasing the amount of value-added work in each process. We also seek to improve efficiency by reducing manpower. Workers freed up by kaizen activity are redeployed. The implicit goal of standardized work is

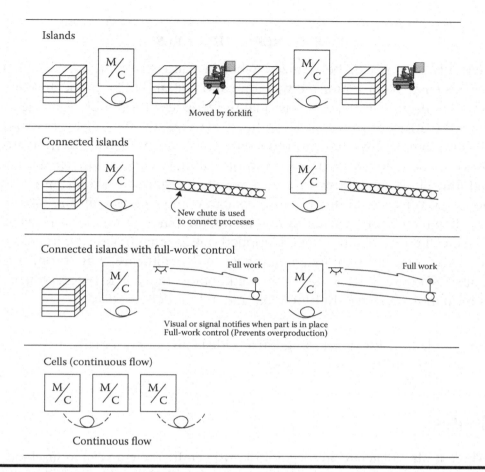

Figure 4.11   Four layout situations.

	Effect				
Type	Efficiency	Lead Time	Quality	Other waste	Comments
Islands (process villages)	Poor	Poor	Poor	Poor	Conveyance muda, scheduling hassles, high WIP, minimal quality feedback.
Connected islands (connected by conveyors, no full-work control)	Somewhat better	Somewhat better	Somewhat better	Somewhat better	Still difficult to adjust to demand changes. Somewhat less WIP (as much as conveyor can hold).
Connected islands— (full-work control)	Somewhat better	Better	Better	Better	Less WIP and conveyance muda.
Cells (continuous flow)	Good	Good	Good	Good	Least WIP, conveyance and motion muda. Continuous quality feedback.

Figure 4.12   Assessment of different layouts.

THE BENEFIT OF CELLS

Great advantages can be realized when a team works in a cell. For a start, it's easy to communicate with one another, and to help one another. Secondly, there is instantaneous quality feedback from your team member in the adjacent process: "Hey, this thing doesn't fit!" Thirdly, because cells are compact, we have to reduce our work in process, which means proportionately lower lead times and operating expenses. Finally, a team working elbow to elbow in a cell inevitably starts to cross-train one another. Over time, all team members can come to know all the jobs in the cell, which improves quality and makes for a more humane workplace.

The cell concept is now being applied outside manufacturing in industries as diverse as banking, insurance, and healthcare with promising results (as a basic Internet search would demonstrate). The biggest barrier (as in manufacturing): dysfunctional mental models.

kaizen. Guidelines for developing kaizen ideas are given. Finally, I discussed typical layouts and their relative merits.

Endnotes

1. There is also a latent disrespect for the worker. If I were a veteran machine operator and someone from planning came to videotape me, I would want to smack him in the head.
2. I mean no disrespect to my industrial engineering colleagues who have inherited these assumptions and recognize the need for change. Rather I wish to highlight potential improvement points in a constructive manner.
3. A series of actions that significantly advance a process is called a job element.
4. Discussion with Toyota executive.
5. Japanese Management Association, *Kanban—Just-in-Time at Toyota* (New York: Productivity Press, 1989).
6. Ibid.
7. Full work is achieved by "two-point control" whereby the amount of standard in-process stock between two processes is controlled. Thus, work from the upstream process does not proceed until the downstream process is "empty." This may entail a small amount of buffer stock between processes that allows work to proceed without interruption while a changeover occurs.
8. Ibid.
9. Toyota Motor Corporation, Operations Management Consulting Division, *The Toyota Production System* (Tokyo, 1995).

10. Toyota training document.
11. A process is a series of steps or actions with a clearly defined goal. A process may be thought of as a "job." A job element is an action or group of actions that advance the process.
12. Required quantity or output per day can be estimated as follows:
    Required output per day = Required output per month ÷ Operating days
13. This assumes that takt time equals cycle time and that there are clear start and stop points per process. Their absence is a common cause of the confusion in production areas. You see people milling around the line but they have no frame of reference.
14. The tools used to develop the work sequence are similar to those used by industrial engineers.
15. Ergonomic injuries make up 70% of workers compensation payments in North America (*Accident Facts 1999*, by the National Safety Council).
16. Japanese Management Association, *Kanban—Just-in-Time at Toyota* (New York: Productivity Press, 1989).
17. Toyota training document.
18. Ibid.
19. Ibid.
20. Ibid.
21. Ibid.
22. Ibid.
23. Ibid.
24. Ibid.
25. Ibid.
26. Mike Rother and Rick Harris, *Creating Continuous Flow* (Brookline, MA: The Lean Enterprise Institute, 2001).
27. Eliyahu Goldratt, *The Goal*, 2nd edition (Great Barrington, MA: North River Press, 1992).
28. Japanese Management Association, *Kanban—Just-in-Time at Toyota* (New York: Productivity Press, 1989).
29. Toyota Motor Corporation, Operations Management Consulting Division, *The Toyota Production System* (Tokyo, 1995).
30. Ibid.
31. Toyota training document.
32. Discussion with Toyota executive.

Study Questions

1. Define standardized work.
2. Check three examples of standardized work in your workplace.
   a. Are they simple, visual, and easy to understand?
   b. Who developed them?
   c. Does work adhere to the standard?
   d. How do you know?
   e. If not, why not?
   f. How might your organization improve its approach to standardized work?
3. Do standards change in your workplace? If so, describe the process.
4. How are new team members trained in your organization?
   a. What role does standardized work play, if any?
   b. How might your organization improve its training processes?
5. Find three examples of standardized work in your office.
   a. Are they simple, visual, and easy to understand?
   b. Who developed them?
   c. Does work adhere to the standard?
   d. How do you know?
   e. If not, why not?
   f. How might your organization improve its approach to standardized work in the office?

Chapter 5

Just-in-Time Production

In a period of low economic growth, overproduction is a crime.

Taiichi Ohno

Just-in-time (JIT) production means producing the right item at the right time in the right quantity. Anything else entails muda. Toyota introduced JIT in the 1950s in response to very concrete problems including

- Fragmented markets demanding many products in low volumes
- Tough competition
- Fixed or falling prices
- Rapidly changing technology
- High cost of capital
- Capable workers demanding higher levels of involvement

At Toyota I came to understand that JIT must be supported by the entire Lean system.

Why JIT?

Conventional mass manufacturers "push"[1] the product through the system irrespective of actual demand.[2] A master schedule is made based on projected demand. Daily orders are given to each department to make the parts final assembly will require. Because changeover times are long, large batches are common.

PRODUCTION PHYSICS

To understand the power of JIT we need basic production physics. Little's law is the fundamental equation, the equivalent of Force = Mass × Acceleration in general physics. Little's law applies in both manufacturing and the service industries.

Little's law: Cycle Time = Work in Process (WIP) ÷ Throughput, or
Throughput = Work in Process (WIP) ÷ Cycle Time

DEFINITIONS

■ Throughput is the average output of a production process (e.g., machine, workstation, line, plant) per unit time (e.g., units per hour, patients per day, insurance policies per week).

■ Cycle time (also called average cycle time, flow time, and throughput time) for a given routing is the average time from release of the part or unit of work to its arrival at the end of the routing (e.g., the time it takes for a patient to go through admitting, triage, general assessment, specialist assessment, treatment, and release).

■ Work in process is the inventory accumulated between the start and end points of a routing (e.g., the number of patients between admitting and release).

IMPLICATIONS

■ For a fixed-capacity process, cycle time and WIP are proportional. Thus, if we release twice as much work into our system, cycle time doubles. Moreover, high WIP levels also mean high operating expenses.

■ To increase throughput, we can flood the workplace with WIP (the mass production or batch and queue approach), or we can reduce cycle time by reducing waste (Toyota's approach).

■ No WIP—no throughput. So much for the "inventory-less factory"! Taiichi Ohno was not opposed to inventory; he was opposed to excess inventory, that is, raw materials, work in process, and finished goods in excess of what you need to satisfy customer demand.

RELATED LAWS

■ *The Law of Variability:* Increasing variability inevitably degrades the performance of the production system.

> ■ *The Law of Variability Buffering:* Variability in a production system will be buffered by some combination of inventory, capacity, and time.
>
> The interested reader is referred to Walter Hopp and Mark Spearman's classic text, *Factory Physics* (New York: McGraw-Hill, 2000).

Keeping track of actual inventory levels is difficult. Parts shortages are not uncommon and "just-in-case" supplies are kept to protect against them. Floor and shelf space dwindles, which necessitates larger facilities, and more conveyance equipment and personnel. The large facilities and batches isolate workers and hinder communication.[3]

In the 1970s manual scheduling methods were replaced by computerized material requirements planning (MRP) systems. A good MRP system could keep track of inventory (more or less), order materials, and send instructions to each department on what to make next. But there were still major problems. If all parts were not logged into the system as they proceeded from one production step to the next, errors began to accumulate. Defects, equipment downtime, unscheduled changeovers, and other random events wreaked havoc with the reorder triggers.

As a result, downstream operations often have either too many or too few parts to meet the production schedule. Even the best MRP system loses touch with the actual condition on the shop floor.[4] Often, the MRP system is supplemented by a backup system of expediters who move parts in urgent shortage to the head of the queue in each department and each machine.

MRP systems have become more and more complex. Capacity planning modules have been added to determine machine capacities at each process step so as to identify potential bottlenecks. In the 1990s they evolved into complex and expensive enterprise resource planning (ERP) software that supposedly serves the entire enterprise, including production, logistics, maintenance, quality, and human resources. Actual results have fallen short of expectations and have been especially disappointing in logistics planning.[5]

Sensitive to the shortcomings of push systems, software suppliers have also developed Lean and flow-enabled ERP systems.[6] Do they work any better? Let the buyer beware!

Basic Principles of JIT

Toyota introduced just-in-time production (JIT) in the 1950s and continues to refine it. JIT was first introduced to North America in the 1980s along with quality circles, statistical process control (SPC), and other Japanese innovations. JIT enjoyed a brief bloom in North America then wilted, as the ground proved infertile.

JIT production follows a few simple rules.[7]

1. Don't produce something unless the customer has ordered it.
2. Level demand so that work may proceed smoothly throughout the plant.
3. Link all processes to customer demand through simple visual tools (called *kanbans*).
4. Maximize the flexibility of people and machinery.

Womack and Jones have also defined the supporting concepts of continuous flow and pull.[8]

Continuous Flow

My friend Mary recently went to her doctor for a nagging shoulder injury. She made the appointment some days ahead, arrived at the appointed time, and waited to be seen. The doctor saw her about an hour later but couldn't make a diagnosis. The doctor decided to send Mary to a specialist.

A few weeks later Mary went through the same routine with the specialist. Mary suggested an MRI. The specialist disagreed and sent her for more X-rays, which took another week. The results were inconclusive. The specialist decided to book an MRI.

After her MRI Mary made another visit to the specialist. Same routine as before. The specialist was finally able to make a diagnosis and prescribed physiotherapy and some drugs. Mary went to her local pharmacy and lined up to get the drugs. She also booked her first physiotherapy session for the following week.

The process took two months, even though the actual time spent receiving treatment was only a few minutes.[9] Most of the time Mary was sitting and waiting (patient is the correct word). Had she been unlucky enough to require hospitalization, she would have entered a whole new world of specialization, disconnected processes, and waiting. Had Mary complained, she would have been told that all this stopping, starting, and waiting, as well as being handed off to strangers is the most efficient way of providing high-quality healthcare.[10] No doubt hospital administrators could produce charts showing that specialist and equipment utilization rates were very high.

This is the world of batch and queue production.

How can we make things flow? Here is a good way to start:[11]

1. Define value from the point of view of the customer.
2. Move machinery and people close together so that they can provide value continuously.
3. Subordinate everything to 1 and 2.

What would this mean for Mary and her sore shoulder? First of all, her doctor and hospital would have to rethink everything from the patient's perspective. They would have to ask:

■ What is of value to Mary?
■ What is waste to Mary?
■ How can we arrange our activities to maximize value and minimize waste?

The answers are obvious:

■ Mary wants a clear diagnosis and quick treatment.
■ Everything else is waste.
■ We should move each process—doctor, specialist, X-ray, MRI, pharmacy, and physiotherapy—closer together and eliminate the obstacles that hinder the flow of value.

This cuts across traditional boundaries of jobs, careers, departments, and organizations. Most managers imagine that goods and services move through the system and that good management comprises minimizing variations in the performance of the complex system. But the real need is to get rid of the system and start over, on the basis of value.[12]

Pull

Pull means that nobody upstream should produce a good or service until the customer downstream asks for it. In the most common type of pull

FLOW AND MUDA

Muda is usually a symptom of obstacles to flow. For example, WIP in front of a machine means that there may be a problem with

- Changeover time (e.g., changeovers are so long that the operator makes as many pieces as possible).
- Machine availability (e.g., machines are unreliable and the operator makes extra parts just in case).
- Quality (e.g., the defect rate is high and the operator has to make more to meet the production target).

Can you think of other examples?

system the customer withdraws the product and we plug the gap created thereby. Applying the pull concept is a little more complicated. Let's look at an example.[13]

For example, suppose you back your blue 2000 Toyota Camry into a post. You go to your local Toyota dealer who installs a blue 2000 Toyota Camry bumper. This creates a "hole" in the dealer's stores area. The hole generates a signal to the local Toyota Parts Distribution Center (PDC): "Please send us a blue 2000 Toyota Camry bumper (to replace the one that we put on the customer's car)."

PDC sends a replacement bumper to the dealer and a signal upstream to the Parts Redistribution Center (PRC), where Toyota suppliers ship their parts. PRC sends a blue 2000 Toyota Camry bumper to the PDC and a signal to the bumper manufacturer: "Please make us a blue 2000 Toyota Camry bumper." The bumper manufacturer schedules a slot of production time to make the blue bumper. Figure 5.1[14] shows the three "pull loops" between the bumper manufacturer and the dealer.

What's the big deal? Well, without the pull system the dealer would have had to carry large parts stores. The PRC and PDC would have had to carry immense warehouses with the associated muda and high costs. Nor would this have ensured quick delivery. The larger the warehouse, the harder it is to keep track of parts. If your bumper were a custom order, you probably would have had to wait several weeks for the bumper manufacturer to make one and the system to deliver it to the dealer.

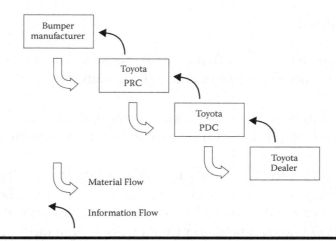

Figure 5.1 Pull through three loops.

The money freed up by the pull system can be used by the dealer to invest in more repair bays, better diagnostic equipment, or training to strengthen the capability of shop mechanics. Similarly, the money saved by the PDC and PRC can be used to strengthen the company further, or to improve the bottom line.

THE MAGIC OF PULL

Pull systems control WIP. The number of kanban cards, bins, footprints on the factory floor, and the like, put an upper limit on WIP in the system. And this in turn:

- Reduces cycle time: In accord with Little's law.
- Reduces operating expense: We aren't ordering as much raw material or making as much WIP and finished goods inventory.
- Improves quality: Defects are not reproduced in large batches, and are easier to catch quickly.
- Improves ergonomics: Part bins aren't as big or numerous so there is less heavy lifting.
- Improves safety: There are fewer forklift trucks whizzing by.

In a pure push system, there is no upper limit on WIP. If an MRP-generated schedule is followed literally, that is, with no adjustment for shop floor conditions, there could easily be a WIP explosion, wherein the schedule gets far ahead of production and buries the plant in WIP.

The JIT System

At Toyota I came to see the essence of JIT: make value flow so that the customer can pull. The components of the JIT system are:

- *Kanban:* A system of visual tools (usually signal cards) that synchronize and provide instruction to suppliers and customers both inside and outside the plant.
- Production leveling or *heijunka*: This supports standardized work and kaizen. The goal is to produce at the same pace every day so as to minimize the peaks and valleys in the workload. Paradoxically, heijunka also supports quick adaptation to fluctuating demand.

Kanban and heijunka in turn depend on

1. Quick machine changeovers, which allow rapid response to daily customer orders and minimize muda of waiting.
2. Visual management through the 5S system, which makes the production condition transparent to the entire team and coordinates action.
3. Capable processes, which means capable methods, workers, and machines:
   a. Capable methods means standardized work, which provides a baseline for kaizen. It also means applying jidoka to both minimize and contain defects.
   b. Capable workers means multiskilled problem solvers who rotate from job to job and are involved in improvement activities.
   c. Capable machinery means TPM and 5S activities that attack the six big losses (equipment breakdowns, setup and adjustment delays, idling and minor stoppages, reduced speed, process defects, and reduced yield).

We have discussed 5S, TPM, and standardized work in some detail. Let us investigate kanban and production leveling.

Kanban

A kanban is a visual tool used to achieve JIT production.[15] Usually, it is a card in a rectangular vinyl envelope. A kanban is an authorization to produce or withdraw and may also contain related information such as

■ The supplier of the part or product
■ The customer
■ Where to store it
■ How to transport it (i.e., the size of the container and the method of conveyance)

Other forms of kanban include

■ An open space on a production floor that indicates to us that someone has withdrawn a product and we must fill the gap.
■ A line on a conveyor or storage rack. When inventory falls below the line, replacement parts are produced.
■ An open space on a conveyance dolly. We produce as many parts as the dolly will hold.
■ An empty parts bin with spaces for a requisite number of parts.
■ An electronic signal from a limit switch to an automatic machine instructing the machine to start producing parts until the "customer is full."[16]
■ A light on a production control board.
■ A space on a parts cart (useful for assembling part kits).
■ A colored ping-pong ball that rolls down a chute when a customer withdraws an item, telling us to "make one of these please."

An electronic message on a computer screen can also serve as a kanban. However, such electronic kanbans do not satisfy the visual management triangle discussed in Chapter 3. This situation may change as computer technology advances and large screens are available that everyone can see at the same time.

There are two kinds of kanban:

■ Production kanban, which specifies the kind and quantity of product that the upstream process (supplier) must produce.
■ Withdrawal kanban, which specifies the kind and quantity of product that the downstream process (customer) may withdraw.

These work in tandem, as illustrated in Figure 5.2.[17] The assembly line makes items *A*, *B*, and *C* using parts *a*, *b*, and *c*. The assembly line "purchases" the specified type and quantity of parts *a*, *b*, and *c* at the parts store

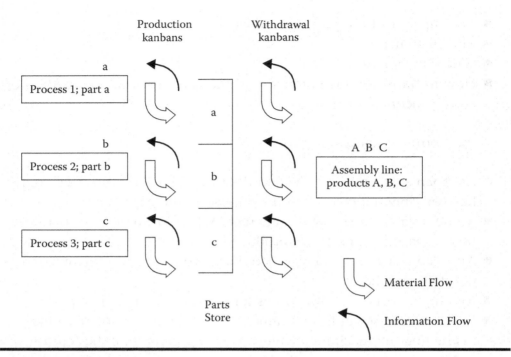

Figure 5.2   Kanban circulation.

using withdrawal kanbans. The resulting gap generates a production kanban for processes 1, 2, and 3, which produce replacement parts to plug the gap.

Withdrawal and production kanbans are exchanged at the supplier process. Parts and products always travel with a kanban. We only produce what has been withdrawn and in the order it was withdrawn. We never ship defects.

What if the parts store ran out of part a? The customer would hand the withdrawal kanban to process 1, which would schedule the work and fill the order. See Figures 5.3 and 5.4.

Storage Area _____ Part No. _____	Process
Item Name _____	
Product Type _____	
Quantity/container _____ Box Type _____	Welding SB-4
Delivery Area _____ Card No. _____	

Figure 5.3   Production kanban.

Stores Shelf _____ Item No. _____	Preceding Process
Item Name _____	
Product Type _____	
Box Capacity _____ Box Type _____	Subsequent Process
Card Number _____	

Figure 5.4   Withdrawal kanban.

PULL AT THE IMPERIAL GRILL—PART 1

My dad's restaurant, the Imperial Grill, used a simple pull system. Waiters and waitresses recorded customer orders on chits (kanbans) which they passed through the serving window. The scheduler, Mama, would determine the best mix and sequence, and post the chits accordingly on the cork scheduling board.

The kitchen (production floor) comprised separate counters (work cells) for

- High-volume and high-frequency orders such as burgers, sandwiches, and salads (runners and repeaters)
- Low-volume orders (strangers or "cats and dogs")

For "high runners," Dad would build up a finished goods buffer, in advance of the breakfast, lunch, and dinner rush, "Cats and dogs," that is, unusual requests, were made to order, a topic of intense debate in the kitchen.

Mama: "Why are we offering steak tartare? Dr. Nagy is the only one who orders it."

Dad: "Yes, but he's a good customer and he sends his patients here."

Kanban Metaphors

At Toyota I learned many kanban metaphors. A kanban is

- The authorization to produce or withdraw parts or finished goods.
- Money. No money means no production.
- The voice of the customer saying, "Please make me..."
- A system of gears that synchronizes production with the "pacemaker process."

The gear metaphor is especially powerful. Mechanical gears synchronize the movement of disparate parts with that of the central motive force. Similarly, kanbans synchronize disparate production processes with the "pacemaker." Only thus can the customer pull through the pacemaker process.

DOES TOYOTA HAVE A PRODUCTION PLAN?

Does JIT production mean you don't need a production plan? In fact, Toyota has long-term, annual, and monthly production plans. These are based on dealer orders in hand and estimated demand over various timeframes. Production plans help to determine personnel and parts requirements and to confirm that there is adequate capacity to meet customer demand. The various forecasts are refined into a 10-day order and then into a daily production plan. Toyota expects changes to the 10-day order in the range of +/−10%. This critical fine-tuning is done with kanbans.

Toyota's daily production plan is given to the pacemaker (usually assembly). Stamping, welding, and painting, as well as suppliers are connected to the pacemaker with kanbans.

Pacemaker Process

The pacemaker is the point of connection with the customer, the process at which production is scheduled.[18] Upstream of the pacemaker, production is determined by the kanban system. For example, suppose the daily customer order is 100 each of products *A*, *B*, and *C*. This order becomes a production kanban for the pacemaker, which will then consume parts from upstream processes as required. Upstream processes will produce parts consumed in pull loops like those shown in Figures 5.1 and 5.2.

The kanban system requires only one production schedule, a tremendous advantage. Thus, the inevitable changes in customer demand and other sources of instability can be accommodated much more easily. With a push system, by contrast, we must schedule and reschedule each point in the production process, which can take days or weeks. The ease of scheduling frees up supervisors and managers for kaizen activity.

Visibility is another big advantage. Kanbans piling up on our production control board mean that we are behind; the customer is ordering stuff and we are not producing it. By contrast, if our board shows fewer kanbans than our minimum level, it means we should stop producing that part.

The Store

In Figure 5.2 we placed our finished parts in a "store" or supermarket. This is where our customers come to "buy" parts.[19] A store is a controlled inventory of parts that is used to schedule an upstream process through some kind of kanban. As we show, one of our kanban rules is that no defective item shall be sent to a customer (whether internal or external). This is the same as a store owner's pledge not to sell a defective product to his or her customers.

Our ideal condition is not to have a store and to practice one-piece production. But this isn't always possible for the following reasons:

- *Cycle time mismatches*: Some processes (e.g., stamping) operate at very fast cycle times and need to change over to serve multiple product families. Others (e.g., injection molding, heat-treating, and dyeing) operate at very slow cycle times and require frequent changeover. One-piece flow is not realistic in such cases.
- *Distance*: Some processes (e.g., those at supplier facilities) are far away and shipping one piece at a time is unrealistic.
- *Process instability or long lead-time*: Some processes are too unreliable to couple directly with other processes in a cell. Others have too long a lead time to be part of a cell.

In the long term we may be able to replace our monuments (large complex batch-producing machinery) with simpler single-piece-flow equipment.[20]

5S and visual management at the store will give us the information we need:

- Where is it?
- What is it?
- How many are there?
- Which one should we produce now?
- How many should we produce?
- Where does it go when we produce it?

Our production condition will be transparent. Too many items may mean that capacity has been raised excessively or that we have quality or machine problems. A store that is practically empty may mean that our capacity is inadequate and that we may be overworking our team members.

KANBAN AND DIRECT BINARY CONNECTIONS

Kanbans are a good example of direct binary supplier–customer connections, which are central to defining value. Manufacturing kanban, for example, contain the following binary tests:

- Did we get the right parts, in the right number and sequence, and at the right time?
- Did the parts meet our quality specification?
- Did we receive our parts in the specified container and conveyance method, and at the right location?

If there's a problem, we know about it at once.

Six Kanban Rules[21]

Team members and supervisors must have a deep understanding of these rules as well as good problem-solving skills. Murphy's Law rules during kanban implementation.

Rule 1: Never Ship Defective Items

Making defects means investing labor, materials, and time into something that we can't sell. Defects seriously impair our ability to reduce cost, our primary goal.
Rule 1 necessitates

- Quick detection and containment of defects, also known as zone control.
- Autonomation (i.e., machines stop automatically when a defect is detected).
- Quick problem solving.
- Where bad parts are mixed with good, we must immediately exchange them for good parts.

Rule 2: The Customer Withdraws Only What Is Needed

We have already discussed this concept in the context of JIT. Our thinking must undergo the critical shift from that of supplying our customer[22] to that of our customer comes to withdraw at the time needed and in the quantity needed. This way of thinking solves the critical problems of production:

- What do we make?
- How many do we make?
- When do we make them?

Corollaries to rule 2 are as follows:

- No withdrawal of goods without a kanban.
- A kanban accompanies each item.
- Withdraw only the indicated parts in the indicated quantity.

Thus, we avoid the muda created when we produce too many, or too early, or the wrong part. These losses can include excess overtime, inventory, and capacity build because we don't know that our existing capacity is sufficient.

Rule 3: Produce Only the Quantity Withdrawn by the Customer

Rule 3 is inferred from rule 2 and allows production processes to function in unison, as if they were part of an assembly line moving at a uniform pace. Kanbans are the gears connecting customer and supplier processes. Corollaries to rule 3 are

- Do not produce more than the number of kanbans in hand.
- Produce in the sequence that you received the kanbans.

We must design our production scheduling boards such that the sequence and quantities are transparent.

Rule 4: Level Production

To allow our processes to produce the right part in the right quantity in the right time, we must give them stability in production orders. We cannot order 50 pieces one hour, then 250 the next. This would require the process to either maintain excess capacity or produce ahead of time. Indeed, the earlier in the production sequence a process sits, the more excess capacity would be required to maintain throughput. We must withdraw product at fixed times, in fixed quantities, and in a fixed sequence. Production leveling is discussed in greater detail later in this chapter.

Rule 5: Use Kanban to Fine-Tune Production

The kanban system cannot respond to major changes in production. These must be addressed in the production plan. Kanban is a means for fine-tuning. For example, if the customer withdraws pieces at an unstable rate—say, 100 pieces in the first hour, 200 pieces the second hour, 75 pieces the third hour—we are likely to start stocking supplies and inventory and invest in excess capacity (people and machinery) just in case, resulting in the collapse of the kanban system.

Rule 6: Stabilize and Strengthen the Process

We cannot satisfy rules 1 to 5 without robust processes. Thus, we must apply the jidoka principle to raise the capability of our processes (see Chapter 6). We seek to continually reduce muda, mura, and muri by

- Implementing poka-yokes to detect errors that might lead to defects
- Reducing walk time or awkward postures that strain our team members
- Rationalizing layouts so that, for example, processes are U-shaped and team members can check the whole process
- Implementing visual systems that reduce cognitive strain

DOES KANBAN APPLY OUTSIDE OF MANUFACTURING?

The kanban concept applies anywhere there's a supplier and customer. Earlier in this chapter I described kanban in a restaurant. Here are few more nonmanufacturing examples.

HEALTHCARE
Post-ICU Beds

Suppose we're a short stay unit in a major hospital. Our internal customers include the post-operating room intensive care unit (ICU). Long stays in an ICU adversely affect the patient, family members, and the hospital. We want the patient out of there as soon as possible.

We could use a kanban to signal when we have a bed available. It could be a physical or electronic "card" containing the following information:

■ Which bed is available, and in what room
■ What type of bed is available
■ When the bed will be available
■ Where to store the bed
■ How to transport the bed and/or the patient (e.g., special instructions on pathways to take or to avoid, how to move the patient and so on)

The six Kanban rules would apply, of course. We would seek to continually strengthen the process.

Operating Room Materials

Suppose we are the operating room team. How will we replenish materials on our anesthetic and intravenous solutions carts? Would it not make sense to (a) apply 5S to make cart min/max levels visible, and (b) use kanban to create direct binary connections between us and the supplier?

KANBAN IN AN OFFICE

Office environments are full of printers and computers, which regularly need work. Printers, for example, run out of ink. A kanban process can reduce printer downtime, ink inventory levels, and unnecessary trips to the office supply store. Similarly, desktop or laptop computers regularly break down. By using kanban and a visual board (e.g., a funnel or pipeline), the IT team could make the following visible: status of a given repair request, workload per team member, and open capacity. Indeed, the same thinking applies to any support team, including design, engineering, research and development, and legal.

Expanded Role of Conveyance

In the JIT system, conveyance workers must convey information as well as materials.[23] Let us look at Figure 5.2 again, which depicts a simple picture: assembly pulls parts a, b, and c from one store. In practice, however, assembly might require parts from several different stores. Conveyance, therefore,

Conveyance	Production
Pitch = parts per container × takt	Takt
Walk route	Work sequence
Parts being conveyed	Standard in-process stock

Figure 5.5   Elements of standarized work—conveyance and production.

would have to put together the necessary kits based on the kanbans submitted and deliver them just-in-time according to a standardized route. Indeed, standardized work for conveyance processes corresponds closely to that for production processes (Figure 5.5[24]).

Pitch determines the frequency of withdrawal, and is a multiple of takt time. For example, if a part has a takt time of one minute and there are 10 parts per tray, the pitch will be 10 minutes.

How Frequently Should We Provide Production Orders?

This is the same as asking, "How big should our lots be?" In the long term our goal is one-piece withdrawal, which means that withdrawal frequency is the same as takt. In the shorter term our goal is to continually reduce lot sizes. Our pitch will be the number of parts in the box multiplied by the takt time.

Let's review the advantages of producing in smaller lots and withdrawing consistent increments of work.

Quick Adjustment to Demand Changes or Other Sources of Instability

Suppose that the supplier process produces batches of 100 units in anticipation of a corresponding demand. But actual demand turns out to be only 50 units. All that work is wasted and the supplier is left holding 50 unsold units in storage.

The mistake was making batch sizes of 100. Had the batch size been 10 or 5, the supplier could have stopped production when it learned that only 50 units would sell.

Better Sense of Takt Time

Small frequent pulling helps us to find the pace of production (i.e., gives us a good takt image). Thus, our situation is easy to monitor: "We were behind. Now we are on our pace."

Fewer Peaks and Valleys

Small lots and small consistent pulling means we require less adjustment. We can do our work evenly without the peaks and valleys that can strain our people, machines, and suppliers. Halving our lot size, for example, means we can halve our parts WIP, thus smoothing the burden for our suppliers.

Abnormality Control

Taiichi Ohno likens manufacturing to the cattle drives of his favorite westerns.[25] Cattle drives involve a small number of cowboys moving thousands of animals hundreds of miles. Under normal conditions the cowboys do little but follow the herd. But if the herd starts to stray off course, the cowboys quickly move to the head of the pack and correct the course. If a few animals continue to stray the cowboys use their lassos to return them to the pack. Cowboys must frequently check the herd's course and take quick action when there is an abnormality. Similarly, frequent production orders support by-the-minute checking and corrective action.

Two Kinds of Conveyance

There are two kinds of conveyance in the kanban system:[26]

- Fixed time and variable quantity conveyance
- Fixed quantity and variable time conveyance

Fixed time conveyance is preferable when processes are disconnected and conveyance distances are long. Easy to follow or "milk run" routes can be readily set up. External suppliers almost always use this form of conveyance.

Discussion Point	Fixed Time	Fixed Quantity
Inventory	Supplier must adapt to variable quantities	Supplier must adapt to variable times
Withdrawal time	Fixed	Variable
Quantity withdrawn	Variable	Fixed
Usage	Disconnected processes Long conveyance distances	Connected processes Short conveyance distances Large-lot production
Metaphor	City Bus Service	On-call taxi service

Figure 5.6   Fixed time versus fixed quantity conveyance.

Fixed quantity conveyance is preferable when processes are connected (e.g., an assembly line) and conveyance distances are short, or when lot sizes are large (e.g., stamping). Toyota uses fixed quantity conveyance for stamped parts and for large injection-molded parts such as instrument panels (see Figure 5.6).

Production Leveling

Most assembly departments find it easier to schedule long runs of one product type and avoid changeovers. But we end up paying heavily. Lead times expand because it becomes difficult to serve customers who want something different than the batch we are making now. Therefore, we have to invest in our finished goods store in the hope that we'll have what the customer wants on hand.

Batch production also means that we consume raw materials and parts in batches, which swells WIP inventories. Quality suffers because a single defect becomes replicated throughout the batch. Workers experience unevenness—that is, some lines are busy, others idle—which also degrades efficiency. The unevenness in the work creates strain, which corrodes safety and morale.

Production leveling or heijunka means distributing the production volume and mix evenly over time. For example, instead of assembling all the type A

UNDERSTANDING CUSTOMER DEMAND

To understand customer demand we need to understand:

- *Volume:* How does it change over time? Are there predictable peaks and troughs (e.g., Valentines Day, Mother's Day, and the holiday season)? Is our business seasonal? Simple runcharts of demand are a useful tool. Moving-average charts can also be helpful where demand seems particularly chaotic.
- *Mix:* What products and services comprise the volume? Product-quantity analysis is a most useful tool. It entails making a bar chart of the quantity of each product sold. We usually find that 20% of the products comprise 80% of the volume (the Pareto principle).
- *Variation:* How variable is demand for each product? It's useful to plot the coefficient of variance (COV) of the demand for each product. (COV is defined as the standard deviation divided by the mean.)

We can then use our volume, mix and variation analysis to categorize our products as follows:

- *Runners:* High-volume and high-frequency orders with low variation in demand (e.g., COV less than 1). We might wish to use dedicated lines for Runners.
- *Repeaters:* Moderate volume and order frequency, and moderate variation in demand (e.g., COV of 1 to 1.5). We might wish to group Repeaters with similar parts and produce them in work cells
- *Strangers ("cats and dogs"):* low-volume, low-frequency orders with high demand variation. We'd likely make these to order.

products in the morning and all the type B products in the afternoon, we would alternate small batches of A and B.

It took me a while to grasp the benefits of heijunka. But the more we level the production mix at the pacemaker:

- The shorter our lead time
- The smaller our finished goods and WIP inventory required
- The less unevenness and strain experienced by our operators

In fact, the kanban system is predicated on production leveling, as is standardized work.

Production leveling also helps us determine our personnel, equipment, and material needs. Suppose the amount of work varies as shown in Figure 5.7.[27] If we set our capacity for peak demand, there will be underutilization during

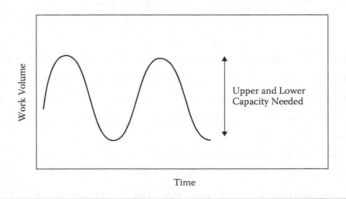

Figure 5.7   Peaks and valleys in work.

valleys. If we set our capacity for our valleys, our people, equipment, and suppliers will experience strain during peak demand.

Responding to Changes in Customer Demand

How do we adjust to ever-changing customer demand? We have three options (in order of preference):[28]

- Absorb day-to-day demand changes with a finished goods store.
- Run a little overtime each shift or the occasional Saturday.
- Adjust our takt time, as required, and toggle the number of operators.

PRODUCTION LEVELING AT THE IMPERIAL GRILL

My dad's place had substantial heijunka challenges. There were three busy periods—breakfast, lunch, and dinner—and long idle gaps. We either had too many people or too few, too much stock or too little. How to level the work? Dad came up with the following ideas:

- Promote mid-morning and mid-afternoon brunches.
- Promote an early evening "happy hour."
- Develop a take-out business.

Things improved, though there were still idle periods, during which I leafed through our *Life* magazine collection.

The first two options can be used daily with little difficulty. Adjusting our takt time as we toggle operators is difficult because we must also change standardized workcharts and retrain and redeploy people. Veteran Lean facilities are adept at such activity, but facilities new to Lean production may struggle initially. We should maintain our new takt time for at least a month.

Fortunately, Lean cells typically use small, simple, and inexpensive equipment that supports flexible responses to customer needs. When we are designing our layouts, we should prepare one-up and one-down scenarios in anticipation of changing takt times.

At Toyota we handled small variations in demand by running a little overtime each day or the occasional weekend shift. We handled larger seasonal variations by adjusting our takt time. We prepared by developing standardized work in advance for different takt scenarios.

		Time (Volume)							
Customer	Product	1	2	3	4	5	6	7	8
Ford	A	O		O		O		O	
Ford	B		Δ			Δ			
GM	C				Φ				Φ
	Total	O	Δ	O	Φ	O	Δ	O	Φ

Figure 5.8   Heijunka box—type A pull system.

Heijunka Box

This is a production-scheduling tool that tells us visually when, what, and how many to build. The production scheduler usually loads the heijunka box with withdrawal kanbans based on that day's order. In a type A pull system the rows and columns of the heijunka box (shown in Figure 5.8) correspond to the

- Number of products the plant or section makes (rows)
- Takt time or pitch

In a type B pull system, the heijunka box usually has only one row and is used primarily to sequence production based on component parts required. Type C systems use both type A and B heijunka boxes.

In this case products Δ and Φ take longer to produce than product O. Loading the heijunka box as shown helps to balance the work. If the Δs or Φs were not scheduled, workers would struggle to maintain takt and standardized work.

DO JIT PRINCIPLES APPLY IN THE OFFICE?

Takt, flow, pull, and Little's law: do these and other JIT principles apply in the office?

Takt can help us understand bottlenecks in, say a promotional marketing process. Suppose our team is required to launch 12 promotional campaigns in a year. Our takt time would be 1 month (12 months divided by 12 campaigns). If we were consistently late, we could develop a balance chart (as in Figure 4.7) to help us identify the bottleneck process. "Aha, our printing process is the bottleneck! Its cycle time is 6 weeks—more than takt."

Flow and pull are extremely helpful in design, engineering, maintenance, and even legal processes. Suppose we're a patent law team in a large organization. Let's say our demand comprises X Runners, Y Repeaters, and Z Strangers. And let's suppose the process comprises steps 1 to 6, (without getting into process details). With good visual management (e.g., a pipeline image, as described in Chapter 3, the section, "Lean in the Office") we can make flow visible. Are our briefs moving? If not, where are they bunching up? Are any lawyers overloaded? Do any lawyers have spare capacity?

Flow, throughput, and lead time invariably improve.

Three Types of Pull Systems[29]

Choosing the right pull system is an important part of Lean implementation.

Type A Pull System

Type A systems are the most common and require replenishing or plugging gaps created in the finished goods or parts store when the customer withdraws a part or product. Kanban cards provide the production authorization and sequence through a heijunka box.

The finished goods store is located at the end of the production line. The size of our finished goods store depends on the rates of production and withdrawal. All parts required to make the goods are stored in the production area, often in a small store. Again, the volume of line-side parts depends on the rates of production and withdrawal.

Type A systems work best when customer orders are frequent and lead times are short and stable (as in the auto parts industry). They require some finished goods and WIP inventory. Our challenge is to strengthen our capability so that we can continually reduce inventory. Indeed, the size of our WIP and finished goods stores is inversely proportional to the capability of our processes.

Type B Pull System

Type B systems are used when order frequency is low and customer lead time is long (e.g., custom producers). The pacemaker is usually farther upstream than in type A systems. Downstream work proceeds sequentially through FIFO (first in, first out) lanes. Kanban cards provide the production authorization and sequence through a type B heijunka box (also called a sequencing box).

To approximate continuous flow in custom processes we must maintain a FIFO flow through each process step and carefully regulate the quantity of work released through the FIFO chain of steps.

Small parts required to make the goods are stored line-side, often in a small store. Large expensive parts are not stored on-site, if possible, to lower inventory costs. Type B systems carry little or no finished goods inventory.

At Toyota Cambridge our assembly line was a B-type system. Parts were supplied by an A-type system. I learned that maintaining the sequence was critical. Failure to do so meant parts all over the shop floor. We had small buffers between departments whose management was an important part of maintaining our sequence.

I came to understand that the size of these buffers is inversely proportional to a plant's capability: the better the plant, the smaller the buffers. Struggling manufacturers often build a separate building wherein they try to patch the sequence back together.

Type C Pull System

Type C systems are a combination of types A and B running in parallel. High-frequency orders are put through the A system; low-frequency orders are put through the B system. Kanban cards provide the production authorization and sequence through both type A and B heijunka boxes. The requirements for each type of pull system apply. Type C systems work best for manufacturers producing both high- and low-frequency items.

PULL AT THE IMPERIAL GRILL—PART 2

The pull system at my dad's restaurant, discussed earlier, entailed

- Replenishment of runners and repeaters (fill-up system)
- Sequential production of strangers (cats and dogs)

"Dad," I told him, after he'd retired, "the Imperial Grill was a classic type C pull system."

He looked over at my mother, "You hear that, Helen? Too much school destroys the mind."

LAW OF UTILIZATION

If an asset's utilization rate increases above 80%, without other changes, cycle times increase exponentially.[30]

Here's an example from daily life. How long does it take to go from downtown Chicago to O'Hare Airport at 3:00 a.m. on a Sunday? Say, 20 minutes or so? How long does that same trip take at 5:00 p.m. on a Friday before a long weekend? Don't ask!

In the former case, highway utilization rates are very low, whereas in the latter they're very high and certainly far above the 80% threshold. Result: cycle times explode, (as do driver stress levels!)

Toyota factories run a maximum of two 10-hour shifts. You'll note this represents a utilization rate of just over 80%. Auto factories are billion-dollar assets. You'd think Toyota would run theirs 24-7. But doing so would contravene the law of utilization, at heavy cost.

The law applies to any asset, including engineers, designers, and project specialists! A common failure mode outside the office is "over-filling the hopper" and pushing utilization rates above 100%. The underlying mental model appears to be: "If I push enough stuff into the pipeline, more will come out the other end!"

In fact, the opposite happens. The pipeline turns to cement. Nothing flows, and people burn out.

Value Stream Mapping

Value stream mapping[31] (VSM) is an invaluable tool that helps us grasp our current condition and identify improvement opportunities.[32] VSM is a language comprising the symbols shown in Figure 5.9.[33] A detailed discussion of this VSM is beyond our scope,[34] but Figures 5.10 and 5.11, which are based on an actual Lean implementation, illustrate its power.

Figure 5.10 shows a current-state map for St. Clair Pallet, a commercial pallet manufacturer. The process involves sawing, notching, and assembly of various types of wood. Currently, the production manager schedules production manually at each process based on perceived daily priorities. There are frequent changes to the schedule (shown by the dotted lines). Lead times ranged from 12 to 15 days, and 10% of orders are late.

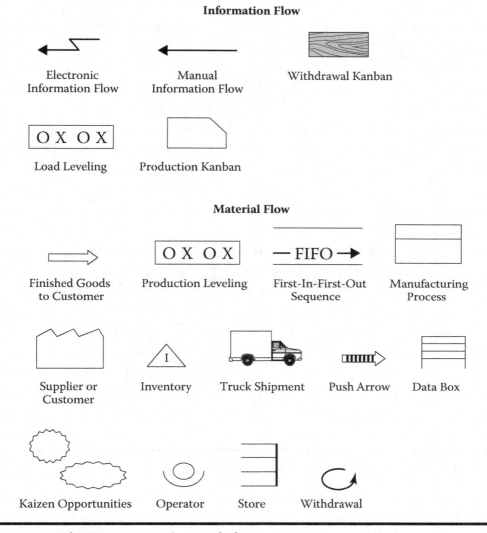

Figure 5.9   Value stream mapping symbols.

Workers are paid a piecework rate and work as fast as they can. Cycle times at assembly are unstable and range from 80 to 120 seconds. Inventories are high in the wood yard and between each process. Changeover time at the multisaw is 30 minutes and at the notching machine is 20 minutes. There is much muda of waiting at each process caused by short parts, machine downtime, and changeovers.

The kaizen opportunities are indicated by the "spiky clouds" and are the basis of our future-state map, shown in Figure 5.11. Some of the planned improvements are

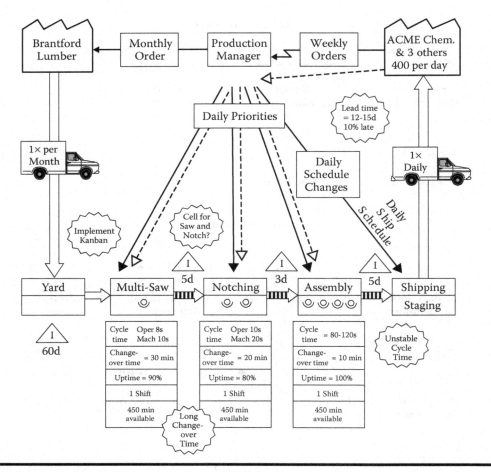

Figure 5.10 Current-state map—St. Clair Pallet.

- Implement a type A pull system using assembly as the pacemaker. Pull items from a finished goods store containing a day's worth of inventory. The store will accommodate emergency orders, which often disrupt the operation. Our takt time will be 68 seconds.
- Combine the multisaw and notching machine in a cell with two operators.
- Implement a store between assembly and sawing and notching and another in the wood yard. Use kanbans to replenish items withdrawn from each store.
- Assign daily scheduling to the production supervisor, which will free up the manager's time for kaizen.

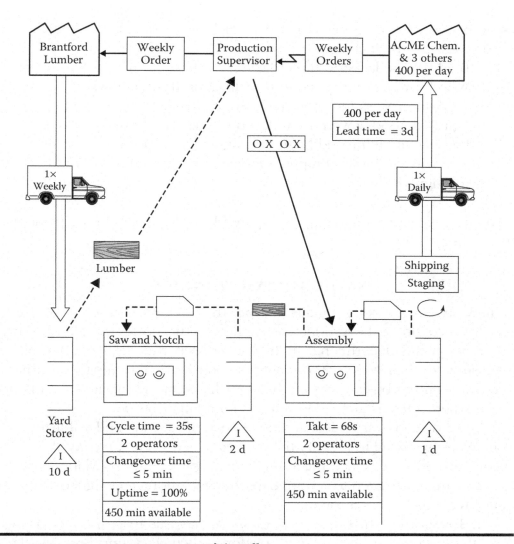

Figure 5.11 Future-state map—St. Clair Pallet.

Many kaizen activities will be required to support the desired future state, including

■ Stabilize the assembly process. Rebalance the work so that two instead of four operators can do it. Reduce assembly changeover times to less than five minutes.
■ Rebalance the saw and notching machine work so two operators can do it in a cycle time of 35 seconds. Reduce changeover times to less than five minutes for each machine.

■ Apply visual management and 5S at each of the stores. The benefits derived thereby include
  – Lead time reduced to three days.
  – Wood yard inventory reduced to 10 days (from 60 days).
  – Work-in-process inventory reduced to two days (from eight days).
  – Finished goods inventory reduced to one day (from five days).
  – Productivity improved by 43% (manpower reduced from seven to four with no loss of output). Operators released thereby will be reassigned.

We also expect to reduce space required by at least 30% in the plant and 50% in the wood yard.

VALUE STREAM THINKING

Value stream thinking entails seeing the combination of processes required to bring the product or service to the customer, rather than process-specific departments. In its absence, departments might optimize measures in their zone without always considering the impact on other areas, or on the business as a whole. Such "point optimization" is often seen where kaizens aren't coordinated for a larger purpose.

As we deepen our understanding of Lean production and stabilize our processes, we need to identify the total value stream that creates the end product or service. Once the value stream is identified, a value stream leader can be assigned to ensure departmental efforts are aligned to produce real results for customers.

In Toyota the "chief engineer" or *shusa* has this responsibility. They are the pacemaker for an auto platform such as Camry or Corolla. Although the chief engineer at Toyota has little formal authority, he or she is acknowledged to be the platform's most powerful person to whom even senior executives defer.

BUSINESS PROCESS VALUE STREAM MAPPING

Every business is a collection of processes. Some are internal (e.g., manufacturing, accounting, hiring, training). Others are shared with other businesses and/or with customers (e.g., purchasing, new product development, product servicing).

Where there is a process, there are value-added steps, and there is waste. Thus, value stream mapping can also help us improve all our business processes. Industries such as healthcare, banking, and insurance are already deriving substantial benefit thereby, and we're only scratching the surface.

Summary

JIT means producing the right part in the right quantity at the right time. The objective of JIT is to produce a continuous flow of value so that the customer can pull. JIT supports quick response to customers, a better sense of takt time, and abnormality control. The JIT system comprises kanban and production leveling or heijunka. I have described the six kanban rules and the three types of pull systems. Conveyance takes on greater importance in the Lean system. Both fixed time and fixed quantity conveyance is possible. Value stream mapping is a language that helps us grasp our current condition and identify kaizen opportunities.

Endnotes

1. "Push" means producing even if there is no demand. "Pull" means you produce only when there is a customer order.
2. Actual demand means a customer order in hand.
3. Traditional manufacturing plants are usually noisy, which exacerbates the communication problem. Lean facilities require quiet machinery so that team members can talk to each other.
4. I wish I had a shekel for every time a shop floor worker has whispered to me, "Our MRP system doesn't work."
5. Sobeys, Canada's no. 2 supermarket chain had to take a $49 million write-down after the company was forced to scrap a $90 million supply chain management software system (*National Post*, June 28, 2001). Shortly thereafter, I spoke at a conference attended by staff from both Sobeys and the software supplier. There were dirty looks, but no gunfire was exchanged.
6. Brian Nakishima, "Can Lean and ERP Work Together?," *Advanced Manufacturing* (September, 2000).
7. Discussion with Toyota executive.
8. James Womack and Daniel Jones, *Lean Thinking* (New York: Simon & Schuster, 1996).

9. We could calculate the percent value-added in this healthcare interaction using the formula (Minutes receiving treatment/Total time elapsed).

10. My Mediterranean temperament limits my tolerance for such stuff. "Helluva way to run a ballroom," I mutter. I focus on prevention so as to avoid the healthcare system entirely.

11. Ibid.

12. Ibid.

13. Ibid.

14. Ibid.

15. Japanese Management Association, *Kanban—Just-in-Time at Toyota* (New York: Productivity Press, 1989).

16. Also called "full work."

17. Ibid.

18. Mike Rother and John Shook, *Learning to See* (Brookline, MA: The Lean Enterprise Institute, 1999).

19. Ibid.

20. "Toyota Must Maintain Edge of Quality as It Tries to Step Up U.S. Production," *Wall Street Journal*, March 20, 2001, contains an interesting case study.

21. Japanese Management Association, *Kanban—Just-in-Time at Toyota* (Portland, OR: Productivity Press, 1986).

22. "Customer" can also mean the process downstream from us.

23. Discussion with Toyota executive.

24. Toyota training document.

25. Mike Rother and John Shook, *Learning to See* (Brookline, MA: The Lean Enterprise Institute, 1999).

26. Discussion with Toyota executive.

27. Japanese Management Association, *Kanban—Just-in-Time at Toyota* (New York: Productivity Press, 1989).

28. Ibid.

29. This section may be beyond the scope of a primer. It may be safely skipped by the newcomer to Lean production.

30. Walter Hopp and Mark Spearman, *Factory Physics* (New York: McGraw-Hill, 2000).

31. At Toyota a value stream map is called a material and information flow diagram.

32. Mike Rother and John Shook, *Learning to See* (Brookline, MA: The Lean Enterprise Institute, 1999).

33. Ibid.

34. Ibid. This book is an excellent resource.

Study Questions

1. Walk a value stream or line of business in your organization (i) in a production (or operations) process, and (ii) in an office process.
   a. What is takt time (or demand)? How visible and understood is takt (or demand) across the value stream?
   b. What triggers production or shipping (or service provision)? How often?
   c. What is the batch size?
   d. What are the main obstacles to flow across the value stream?
   e. How might you improve flow across the value stream?
2. For the value stream(s) you chose in Question 1:
   a. How is demand variation buffered: through inventory, capacity, or lead time? Explain your answer.
   b. How effective are current buffers?
   c. How might your organization improve?
3. Provide at least one example each of Type A, B, and C pull systems, either in your workplace or from daily life.
   a. Any reflections and insights?
4. Draw a value stream map for a product or service family in your organization.
   a. What are the biggest obstacles to flow?
   b. What are possible countermeasures?

Chapter 6

Jidoka

Stop production so that production never has to stop.

Toyota proverb

The Japanese word *ji-do-ka* comprises three Chinese characters. The first, *ji*, refers to the worker herself. If she feels "something is wrong" or "I am creating a defect," she must stop the line. *Do* refers to motion or work, and *ka* to the suffix "-ation." Taken together jidoka has been defined by Toyota as "automation with a human mind" and implies intelligent workers and machines identifying errors and taking quick countermeasures.[1]

At Toyota, I came to understand that jidoka means making defect-free processes by continually strengthening

- Process capability.
- Containment. Defects are quickly identified and contained in the zone.
- Feedback. So that quick countermeasures can be taken.

I also came to understand that jidoka represents a revolution in quality management, which perhaps has yet to be fully grasped.

Development of the Jidoka Concept

Zero defects is absolutely possible.

Shigeo Shingo

Sakichi Toyoda, the company founder, was the first to intuit the jidoka concept. In 1902 he invented a loom that would stop automatically if any threads snapped. This opened the door for automated loomworks in which a single operator could handle dozens of looms.

Sakichi's invention reduced defects and waiting time and raised productivity. Sakichi also introduced the idea that it was OK to stop production to ferret out the root causes of defects.

Shigeo Shingo developed and extended the jidoka concept.[2] But first he had to overcome the quality profession's overemphasis on statistics, fostered ironically by W. Edwards Deming. Indeed, Shingo said that it took him 26 years to escape the spell of the "god of statistical methods."

Our goal, he argued, was to reduce defects. But statistical methods are based on the expectation of defects, and not on their prevention. For example, statistical process control (SPC), which tells us how many defects we'll produce, misses the point. The goal should be to prevent defects. Shingo also observed that SPC:

- Alienates production managers, supervisors, and workers who were responsible for quality
- Is based on the false premise that 100% inspections are impossible

"Why not zero defects?" asked Shingo.

To achieve this outlandish goal he invented a concept called *poka-yoke*,[3] which refers to simple, inexpensive failure-proofing devices. Shingo also developed what he called source inspection to support poka-yokes. Finally, he proved that 100% inspection was achievable at low cost.

Why Jidoka?

Humans are animals that make mistakes.

Shigeo Shingo

High defect rates lead to frequent line stoppages, which make flow and pull impossible. Kanban systems collapse when defective parts are shipped. Productivity implodes; lead times and costs balloon.

Shingo's observation about humans making mistakes was prescient. Data compiled by the US military and aerospace programs has confirmed that humans are often the least reliable components of complex systems.

JIDOKA—THE NEGLECTED PILLAR?

If you do a Google search on the term "just-in-time," you'll get well over a million hits. But if you do a search on the term "jidoka," not so many. JIT is the "glamorous" pillar. But JIT depends on quality. Otherwise, we're just shipping junk faster. Without jidoka, our Lean house begins to tilt and may even come crashing down.

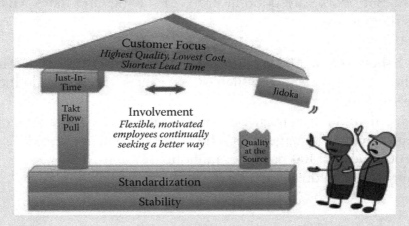

Jidoka essentially means, "Build in quality at the source," and comprises three things:

1. Don't accept defects.
2. Don't make them.
3. Don't pass them on.

A good example of jidoka is Toyota's famous *andon* process, wherein workers are encouraged to stop the line whenever they detect a significant abnormality. At its heart jidoka entails:

■ Direct binary supplier–customer connections
■ Embedded binary tests to signal OK/Not OK.

Taken together, these allow us to

1. Translate our grasp of customer needs into a small number of agreed-upon measures.

2. Put these measures up on a board showing the target versus actual, and a Red/Green assessment.

3. Hold daily stand-up team meetings wherein we discuss hot spots and countermeasures.

Machines are better than people at detecting defects and stopping the process. But people are good at problem solving, and that's what jidoka allows them to do.

Figure 6.1 shows typical human error rates for a variety of tasks. The left side of the scale represents the highest error rates, the right side the lowest human error rates.

Even highly trained military personnel make errors about 20% of the time in simulated military emergencies. The very best humans can do is one error every 10,000 tries, or 100 parts per million.

But the errors needn't turn into defects.

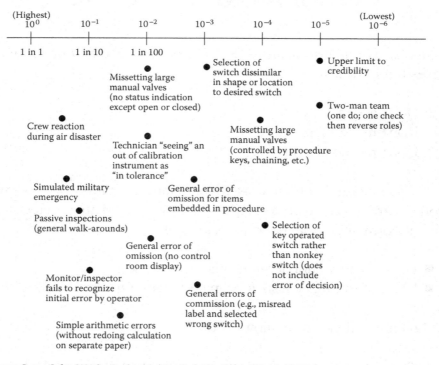

SOURCE: *System Safety 2000*, Joe Stephenson (New York: Van Nostrand Reinhold, 1991).

Figure 6.1 Human error rates. (Courtesy of Lean Pathways Inc., Copyright 2014.)

How to Improve Human Reliability

We already discussed standardized work, visual management, and 5S as ways to improve human reliability. There is another method.

STOP PRODUCTION—SO THAT PRODUCTION NEVER STOPS

That's what we were taught at Toyota. The underlying mental model is "Don't ship junk!", versus mass production's, "Make your numbers! (We can fix them later)."

Our team members were encouraged to identify problems by pulling the so-called andon or help line (normally a cord that runs along the assembly line). During a new model launch, the line stopped all the time, which triggered intense problem solving. We had to get the line going again, by identifying and addressing root causes, thereby improving process capability and containment.

The first few days of a new launch we might only make 10 or 15 units a shift. But very soon we would achieve full production, and sustain it. Our Toyota senseis were mistrustful of production lines with low andon use. Once, during a shop floor report out, a young group leader claimed there were no problems on his line, and thus no andon pulls. The sensei shook his head, "No problem is a big problem."

Poka-Yoke

Poka means inadvertent error, and *yoke* means prevention. *Poka-yoke* means implementing simple low-cost devices that either detect abnormal situations before they occur, or once they occur, stop the line to prevent defects.[4] Shingo was careful to distinguish between errors, which he felt were impossible to avoid, and defects, which he believed could be entirely eliminated.[5,6]

Common Errors

Poka-yokes reduce a worker's physical and mental burden by eliminating the need to constantly check for the common errors that lead to defects. Here are the most common errors in order of importance:

1. Missing process steps (e.g., flux not applied prior to welding)
2. Process errors (e.g., weld applied does not meet standard)

3. Mis-set work pieces (e.g., piece set backward and weld applied to wrong place)
4. Missing parts
5. Wrong parts
6. Wrong work piece processed
7. Faulty machine operation
8. Adjustment errors (e.g., error in cutting machine adjustment leads to part being cut too thin or too fat)
9. Equipment not set up properly
10. Tools and jigs inadequately prepared

A good poka-yoke satisfies the following requirements:

■ Simple, with long life and low maintenance
■ High reliability
■ Low cost
■ Designed for workplace conditions

Shop floor team members are usually the best source of poka-yokes.

Inspection Systems and Zone Control

At Toyota I came to appreciate the concept of "zone control." Each successive management level from team leader, to supervisor, to plant manager was encouraged to think in terms of his or her zone. For example, a team leader's zone was his or her immediate team and work area. The supplier and customer were the upstream and downstream team, respectively. This way of thinking compelled the development of redundant controls, which are the essence of reliability engineering.

Judgment Inspections—Discovering Defects

These are "good–no good" inspections, whose objective is to prevent defects from getting to the customer or to downstream processes. These are postmortem activities often conducted by a separate inspection department,[7] which generally entail little root cause analysis or feedback to the defect source. Judgment inspections do not strengthen our processes or people, and they are wasteful. More effective approaches do exist.

Informative Inspections—Reducing Defects

These are designed to discover defects, as opposed to errors, and to give feedback to the source, which then takes corrective action. Often they entail the use of statistical tools such as sampling protocols and SPC. Informative inspections tend to be superior to judgment inspections, but feedback and countermeasures often lag.

The most effective informative inspections are those that involve self-checking or successive checking.[8] Self-checking means that the operator checks his or her own work. U-shaped cells support self-checking by placing the start and end process side by side. In successive checking the downstream process checks for defects and provides immediate feedback. Such checking should be done peer to peer because supervisor checks can appear to be punitive. At Toyota I found that successive checking can be very effective when it covers 100% of the items. Assembly lines are conducive to this type of checking.

Source Inspections—Preventing Defects

These are inspection methods designed to discover errors that might lead to defects and to give quick feedback to the source. Toyota Cambridge's target was 100% inspection of priority processes. Source inspections can be categorized as vertical or horizontal.

Vertical Source Inspections

These require an upstream search for the root cause. For example, burrs on metal pieces in the assembly shop may have their source in the weld shop. Or a water leak in assembly may be due to improper application of sealant in the paint shop.

The standardized approach to problem solving and strong feedback loops at Toyota allowed us to quickly identify and attack shared problems. These upstream and downstream feedback loops were the key to improving process capability and containment.

Horizontal Source Inspections

These involve seeking root causes within the department. For example, the root cause of wrong and missing defects in an assembly shop is often the absence

CAN WE REALLY JUST STOP THE LINE?

As noted earlier, jidoka comprises three things:

- Don't accept defects.
- Don't make them.
- Don't pass them on.

Don't make defects is perhaps the most difficult and entails the following steps:

1. Detect the defect, or better yet, the error that precedes the defect.
2. Stop the process.
3. Call for help and fix the immediate condition.
4. Solve the problem at root cause, so it doesn't happen again.

People sometimes struggle with step 2. "Can we really just stop the line? We won't make defects, but we also won't make any money!"

Correct! In fact, jidoka entails all four elements. Remember, machines are better than humans at elements 1 and 2, detecting defects and stopping the line. But humans are better at calling for help and solving problems. Our human response system must be quick and effective so we can solve the problem and get the line back up. This requires a good in-advance understanding of possible failure modes and countermeasures. At Toyota, when our andon board lit up and the corresponding music sounded, we had 60 seconds. Believe me, we swarmed the problem!

But what if we couldn't solve the problem in 60 seconds? First, we had to stop the bleeding with temporary countermeasures, usually some form of containment. Then we had a choice: (a) we could pull the unit offline for deeper problem solving, and restart the line, or (b) we could tag the defect and tackle it at the next containment area. It was tough, the constant creative tension between stopping the line to ferret out a defect, and getting the line going again. But that's the price of excellence.

In summary, jidoka entails both human and machine elements. A weak human response system leads to downtime, delay, and frustration.

of techniques that ensure all required parts are installed. The root cause of pits, mars, or other paint defects is often contamination within the paint shop itself.

At Toyota we developed feedback loops between supervisors within each department so that defects were contained and fixed "in the zone." Each supervisor was encouraged to think like a small business owner with suppliers and customers.

Using Poka-Yokes

An effective poka-yoke

- Inspects 100% of the items.
- Provides immediate feedback so as to compel countermeasures. Source inspections (error prevention) are the most powerful poka-yoke. Informative inspections (defect prevention) can be effective, especially when based on self- or successive checking.

Two Types of Action

When a poka-yoke detects an error, it should either shut down the machine or deliver a warning.

Shutdown

These are the most powerful poka-yokes. For example:

- A light sensor stops a drilling operation when it fails to detect the requisite number of holes in the work piece.

- A machine will not start if a work piece is incorrectly positioned. The on switch sends a weak electric current to reference pins, and only when the part makes contact with each pin will the machine start.
- A tapping machine stops because the metal sensor fails to detect a washer at each drilling point.

A final example of the shutdown poka-yoke is the so-called full-work system wherein a supplier process stops feeding the downstream process when it is full (i.e., when the desired number of parts have been provided).

Warning

Warning poka-yokes alert us to abnormalities by activating a buzzer or light. The most famous is perhaps the Toyota andon board, which alerts the group leader to problems by lighting the process number, playing a piece of music, or both.[9] The Toyota andon is engaged when a team member pulls the cord that runs along the line.

The line continues to move until it reaches a fixed position. Because each process has a fixed position, team members are able to complete at least one operating cycle. This greatly reduces the potential for defects created by stopping the line in midcycle.[10]

Three Paths to Poka-Yoke

Poka-yokes can detect deviations in the work piece or work method or deviations from some fixed value.[11]

Work Piece Deviations

This type of poka-yoke uses sensing devices to detect abnormalities in the weight, dimensions, or shape of the product, for example:

- *Weight:* Establish a weight standard and weigh each product using a balance.
- *Dimensions:* Make standards for thickness, inner and outer diameter, and so on, and identify deviations using limit switches, stoppers, jigs, photoelectric eyes, and the like.

- *Shape:* Make standards for angles, number and positions of holes, curvature, and so on, and detect deviations with limit switches, locator pins, interference in chutes, and similar detectors.

Work Method Deviations

This type of poka-yoke uses sensors to detect errors in standard motions, for example:

- A photoelectric sensor counts the number of times a worker's hand breaks the beam in reaching for a part. If the requisite number of counts is not met, parts must be missing.
- A counter counts the number of spot welds made on a work piece. The clamps will not release unless the correct number has been made.

With this type of poka-yoke the work must be organized so that the downstream process cannot proceed unless the upstream process has been completed. For example:

- In drilling and welding, a welding jig should be made that will only hold work pieces that have been drilled.
- When assembling multiple models, photoelectric sensors should be used to detect characteristic model shapes. The sensor can then be linked to parts containers, such that only containers required for the given model will open.

Deviations from Fixed Values

Counters are especially useful in this regard. For example:

- A limit switch can be used to count the number of holes drilled in a work piece.
- Weld tips can be changed when a certain count is reached. A counter stops the welding machines when the requisite count is reached and will not restart until a new tip is installed.

Missing part methods can also be effective. For example:

- If the number of parts in an assembly kit is standardized, leftover parts will indicate omission errors.

Measure critical conditions such as pressure, temperature, voltage, or other process parameters. Work cannot proceed unless the value is in the predetermined range. For example:

- Pressure gauges shut down processes when overpressures or leaks are detected.
- Thermocouples shut down motors when excessive temperatures are detected in bearings.
- Torque wrenches provide torque in a target range and shut down outside the range.

Poka-Yoke Detection Methods

Sensor technology is a rich and expanding area. At Toyota we were limited only by our creativity. Sensors may be classified as contact and noncontact devices.

Contact Sensors

The most common contact sensors are

- *Limit switch and microswitch:* Detect the presence of work pieces, dies, or tools. These cheap and robust sensors are widely applicable.
- *Differential transformer:* Picks up magnetic field changes depending on the degree of contact with the work piece.
- *Touch switch:* Activated by a light touch on antenna section; can detect presence, dimensions, damage, and so on.

Limit switches are invaluable for eliminating pinch points and equipment and product damage caused by equipment and products being struck by something.

Noncontact Methods

These devices detect disturbances in photoelectric beams, the proximity of solid objects, metal passage, fibers, colors, ultraviolet light, infrared light, counting abnormalities, electron beams, dimensions, pressure, temperature, electric current fluctuations, and vibration. Here are some commonly used devices:

- *Photoelectric devices:* Widely used as light screens to ensure machine area is clear before machine engages; also used to count actions, fallen objects, and work piece dimensions.
- *Metal passage detectors:* Used to count the number of screws installed, verify whether a part is ejected from the press, and confirm that safety cages are closed.
- *Temperature:* Thermometers and thermocouples are used to detect changes in temperature of dies, motors, and curing ovens.
- *Pressure:* Pressure gauges detect fluid blockage in pipes and overpressures in engines.
- *Electric current fluctuations:* Widely used in spot welding to check for secondary currents that compromise weld integrity.

Figures 6.2 to 6.5 illustrate actual poka-yokes I have encountered among the scores that I have seen. Shop floor team members developed most of them.

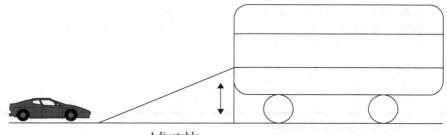

Adjustable
ramp

Industry: Auto manufacturing; **Process:** loading cars in rail cars.
Before Improvement: A car smashed into top of rail car during loading. Rail cars belong to rail firm and their dimensions vary widely.

Poka-yoke
- Cut a piece of wood to the desired length. Label and color code the wood.
- Attach a chain to the wood and make a home position for it.
- Amend standardized work to include height checking.

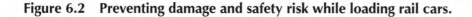

Figure 6.2 Preventing damage and safety risk while loading rail cars.

Industry: Office furniture; *Process:* Drilling & Spot-welding
Before Improvement: Workers occasionally neglected to drill mounting holes on pieces.

Poka-yoke:
• Put a limit switch on the drilling machine
• An alarm sounds if the correct number of holes have not been drilled.

Figure 6.3 Preventing omission of board set mounting holes.

Industry: Welding shop; **Process:** Spot-welding
Before Improvement: Wear and tear necessitates tip changes. When workers occasionally forget to change tips, nuggets slip off specification.

Poka-yoke:
• Add a counter to the spot welder
• When the requisite number of welds have been made, an alarm sounds indicating it is time for a tip change.

Figure 6.4 Confirming spot-welding tip changes.

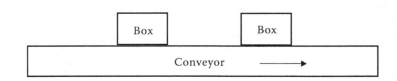

Industry: Consumer product; *Process:* Final packaging.
Before Improvement: Sometimes boxes are not filled due to machine errors, but are closed and shipped anyway.

Poka-yoke:
• Install a pedestal fan by the conveyor.
• Boxes that have not been filled will be blown off the conveyor.

Figure 6.5 Detecting unfilled boxes.

MORE ON POKA-YOKE

Jidoka entails

1. Detect the defect (or the error that precedes it).
2. Stop the process.

3. Call for help and fix the immediate condition.
4. Solve the problem at root cause, so it doesn't happen again.

Poka-yoke is central to steps 1 and 4, and thus improves both process capability and defect containment. Poka-yoke help us catch errors and defects closer to the actual conditions that caused them. Our problem solvers have a better chance of getting to the root cause because process conditions won't have changed much.

Poka-yoke helps ensure the "crime scene," to use a CSI (crime scene investigation) metaphor, hasn't changed when we get there. By contrast, after-the-fact inspection is too late; the crime scene and clues have been spoiled.

Poka-yoke also fosters respect for people. Rather than "rounding up the usual suspects," we look for systemic causes. We recognize our team members want to do a good job, and deserve what Deming called "pride of workmanship." Leaders accept their job is to help team members by reducing hassle and by involving them in improvement activity.

Implementing Jidoka

To continually improve quality, we need a long-term jidoka strategy. I found that Toyota executives thought deeply about questions such as

- How will we measure the capability of each process?
- How will we involve our team members?
- What kind of knowledge will our team members require to make poka-yokes?
- How will we train them?
- What is the role of the team member, supervisor, manager, and executive?
- How will we link jidoka with 5S, standardized work, and TPM?
- How will we communicate and promote jidoka?

I also found that Toyota's hoshin planning process (discussed in Chapter 8) helped to translate these questions into clear focused activities. See Figure 6.5.

Annual Jidoka Strategy and Goals

Jidoka should be part of our broader Lean implementation strategy. Our jidoka plan should address the questions set out in the previous section as well as the following considerations:

- Promotion and communication
- Training
- Measurement and reporting

SMART[12] goals should be set for items such as

- Number or percentage of processes that achieve a specific high rating
- Number of poka-yokes implemented, kaizen circles, suggestions, and the like
- Percentage of team members trained in jidoka
- Percentage of team members involved in jidoka activities

Future Directions

To sustain jidoka our system must compel improvement. We could begin by defining capability and containment levels for our processes. These in turn could be translated into a score and rating for each process, say gold, silver, and bronze.[13]

Our assessment system should be simple and should not depend on statistical methods. The average team member should be able to assess a given process and develop improvement activities. Moreover, the system should itself provide guidance on how to improve from say, bronze to silver, or silver to gold.

JIDOKA OUTSIDE THE FACTORY

Jidoka and its constituent concepts (zone control, poka-yoke, total involvement, etc.) have enormous potential in healthcare, financial services, education, and public service. Consider hospital mis-medications, which are implicated in over 100,000 deaths each year in American hospitals. Here's what a nurse needs to know before delivering a drug intravenously:

- Right patient?

- Right drug?
- Right dose?
- Drug in the correct form (e.g., should it be diluted and administered with a drip IV)?
- Is patient taking other drugs that might make this drug dangerous?

People are not wired for infallibility. Can we expect a nurse or doctor to answer these questions on her own in a crisis at 3:00 a.m.? Jidoka in the form of embedded tests for each question can greatly reduce mis-medication frequency.

Staying in healthcare, hand hygiene is a major factor in the infections that kill tens of thousands of Americans each year. Some hospitals are turning to poka-yokes in the form of buzzers, lights, and other trackers that signal annoyingly when workers fail to sanitize.

Jidoka is also very helpful in the financial services sector. Credit card and mortgage applications, for example, require accurate input of many pieces of information. Poka-yokes can greatly reduce defect levels. Can we not thereby engage the good people doing the work? Jidoka's constraint outside the factory is not technical, but cultural. ("Can we really engage everybody in improving our work?")

Summary

The jidoka concept was invented by Sakichi Toyoda and developed and extended by Shigeo Shingo. Jidoka is essential if we are to achieve our targets of best quality at lowest cost in the shortest lead time. Jidoka requires a fundamental rethinking of quality management, away from statistical quality control, and toward 100% inspection and poka-yoke. A poka-yoke is a simple, inexpensive, and robust tool that inspects 100% of items, detects errors that might lead to defects, and provides quick feedback so that countermeasures can be taken. Team members are the best source of poka-yokes.

Poka-yokes either shut down equipment or provide a warning when an error has been detected. Poka-yokes typically identify abnormalities in product characteristics, differences with respect to a fixed value, or missing process steps. Sensor technology is a rich field that provides unlimited support for poka-yoke development. Sensors can be contact or noncontact type.

We need to develop a long-term jidoka strategy that will support our long-term Lean production implementation strategy. Future directions are suggested for jidoka development.

Endnotes

1. Toyota Motor Corporation, Operations Management Consulting Division, *The Toyota Production System* (Tokyo, 1995).
2. Shigeo Shingo, *Zero Quality Control: Source Inspection and the Poka-yoke System* (New York: Productivity Press, 1986).
3. Ibid.
4. Shingo initially introduced the word *baka-yoke*, which means foolproof, but then changed it to avoid a negative connotation for workers.
5. Shigeo Shingo, *Zero Quality Control: Source Inspection and the Poka-yoke System* (New York: Productivity Press, 1986).
6. *NKS Factory Magazine, Poka-Yoke: Improving Quality by Preventing Defects* (New York: Productivity Press, 1987).
7. Shigeo Shingo, *Zero Quality Control: Source Inspection and the Poka-yoke System* (New York: Productivity Press, 1986).
8. Ibid.
9. Many a Toyota team leader has muttered "I hate that song" while speeding to the problem.
10. For real emergencies Toyota also has an andon that immediately stops the line.
11. Ibid.
12. SMART stands for simple, measurable, achievable, reasonable, and trackable.
13. Discussion with Toyota executive.

Study Questions

1. Assess Jidoka in at least three processes in your organization.
   a. What measures are currently taken to build quality into each process?
   b. How effective are these measures?
   c. How would you improve quality in each process?
2. Define "zone control."
3. Walk a value stream or line of business in your workplace.
   a. Which areas have the most effective zone control, and why?
   b. Which areas have the least effective zone control, and why?
   c. How well is the zone control concept understood and practiced in your workplace?
   d. What might your organization do to improve?
4. Identify at least three poka-yokes in day-to-day life.
   a. What are the embedded tests?
   b. How might you improve these poka-yokes?
5. Identify at least three poka-yokes in your workplace.
   a. What are the embedded tests?
   b. How might you improve the poka-yokes?
6. Describe an andon or line-stop you are familiar with.
   a. What makes the andon effective, or ineffective?
   b. How would you improve the andon?

Chapter 7

Involvement

What a terrible waste of humanity.

Taiichi Ohno

Just as the wind brings a splendid sailboat to life, total involvement animates the Toyota system. Involvement should be managed as intensely as production and quality. As we expanded at Toyota Cambridge we learned to ask questions such as

- How will we involve our team members?
- What skills will they need to become involved?
- How will we support and sustain involvement?
- How will we measure involvement?
- What is the role of management?

These questions informed our culture strategy.

Why Involvement?

It took me a while to grasp the importance of involvement, raised as I was in contemporary business practice. Indeed, I had learned that you should keep people in the dark, especially the union.

Involvement goes against 100 years of management practice. It is anathema to the command and control managers who are perhaps more prevalent than is admitted. How can a shop floor worker whose education and experience are limited contribute to business decisions? Don't inattentive workers cause most production or quality or safety problems?

Taylor's assumptions regarding worker capability are no longer valid. Today's workers are better educated and more literate that ever before. Away from work they have access to unprecedented learning opportunities through community colleges, universities, TV, and the Internet. Moreover, our culture places a premium on creativity and individual expression. "How are you going to keep them down on the farm after they've seen Paree?"

Moreover, today's companies need flexibility and creativity to sail rapidly changing markets, technology, and financial conditions. We are buffeted by difficult problems every day. We need all hands on deck to avoid the rocks and other dangers. Indeed, team member knowledge, experience, and creativity are a motherlode.

ALL HANDS ON DECK

Here's how problems are distributed at most organizations.

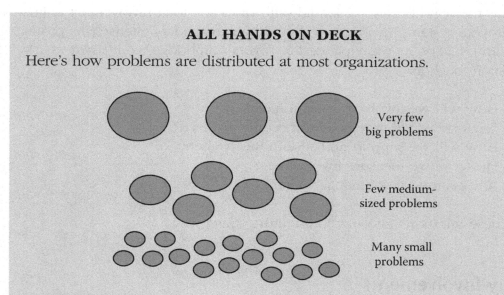

Very few big problems

Few medium-sized problems

Many small problems

To continually improve, we need to engage all our team members, especially those on the front lines, where the real work gets done. Only they can identify and fix the myriad small problems that invariably add up to monster problems.

In the next chapter we discover how to link our frontline involvement and problem-solving activities with our critical few strategic needs.

Terrible Waste of Humanity

A celebrated story[1] from the early 1950s tells how during a visit to a supplier, Taiichi Ohno stopped to observe a process. The operator stood watching his machine. After watching several cycles, Ohno asked him, "How often does this machine break down?"

"Never," the worker replied.

"Well, what do you do all day?"

"I watch this machine, Ohno-san."

"All day long, you watch this machine, which never breaks down?"

"Yes," said the worker, "that is my job."

"What a terrible waste of humanity," thought Ohno.

This was a red-letter day in business history. With this flash of insight Ohno began to bring planning and production together again. You will recall that the Taylor system was based on separating planning from production, which created the dysfunction described in Chapter 1. Ohno, by contrast, sought to engage his workforce in production planning and problem solving. He knew that his system would fall apart without the wholehearted involvement of his team members.

It is easy to be blasé in hindsight. But Ohno and Eiji Toyoda were betting the farm on untested ideas. How did they encourage and support worker involvement? How do we motivate involvement today?

Some have suggested that involvement comes easier for the Japanese because theirs is a more homogeneous and group-oriented society. This may be true, but it is wrong to assume that North American workers resist involvement. In fact, workers at countless North American plants eagerly participate in improvement activities every day. Worker involvement requires mutual respect and hassle-free systems.

Mutual respect means employment security. Workers must have confidence that improvement will not result in job losses. This is all well and good in a greenfield plant, but what about the brownfield plant that is facing shutdown? How can we guarantee employment security there?

Sadly, we can't. But we must be up front about our condition. At the outset of a Lean conversion we must say to our workers, "We can save some of the jobs, or we can save none of them." We should make the necessary cuts in headcount early on through targeted early retirement packages if possible. Once we have reached the optimal size, we must commit to job security and stick to it.

THE ILLUSION OF TOP-DOWN CONTROL

Fred Taylor separated planning from production. Productivity soared, but at a terrible cost. Frontline team members were alienated, and managers were infected with the illusion of top-down control.

The Taylor system fostered mental models such as

- We can manage from a distance, by the numbers.
- What can frontline team members possibly teach us?
- Improvement comes when smart people (just like us) tell frontline people what to do!

Such thinking afflicts us still. It's so engrained that few even think to question it. Our professional and business schools are rife with it. (Henry Mintzberg jokes that newly minted MBAs should have a skull and cross-bones tattooed on their foreheads.[2])

I don't want to be misunderstood. I learned a great deal in engineering and business school. But I also absorbed unhelpful thinking that took a decade to overcome.

Activities Supporting Involvement

5S, TPM, and standardized work are all important involvement channels that we have already discussed. In this chapter we focus on

- Kaizen circle activity
- Practical kaizen training
- Suggestion programs

First, though, it's helpful to understand the goal of involvement.

Goal of Involvement

The explicit goal of all involvement activities is to improve productivity, quality, cost, delivery time, safety and environment, and morale (PQCDSM) by

- Solving specific problems (e.g., improving containment by developing a poka-yoke, reducing walk time by altering layout, reducing changeover time, etc.).
- Reducing hassles (e.g., developing production analysis boards that make the current condition visible to all and applying 5S so that things are easy to find).
- Reducing risk (e.g., by reducing ergonomic burden, eliminating pinch points and other hazards, or implementing poka-yokes to eliminate spills).
- But the deeper goal is to improve team-member capability. We will never be short of problems. By strengthening our people we can confidently face the future.

GETTING STARTED—QUICK & EASY KAIZEN

Everybody is afraid of change; it's how we're wired. Our brain comprises three sections:

- Limbic brain, the oldest "reptilian" part, which controls basic functions including the "fight or flight" response
- Mammalian brain, which contains our emotional center
- Prefrontal cortex, our managerial center

When we face change, the limbic brain kicks in and we feel anxious. The bigger the change, the greater our anxiety.

Quick & Easy kaizen (*kaizen teian* in Japanese) entails small improvements in day-to-day work identified, and implemented, by individual team members. With time, fear subsides and kaizen becomes a habit. Moreover, small changes can add up to big improvements.

Develop a Quick & Easy kaizen system. Use visual management in the form of simple pocket cards and a Quick & Easy kaizen board so everyone can see what's happening. Review ideas during daily team huddles. Keep the approval process simple (e.g., immediate supervisor approves) for volume and speed.

If you stick with it, a benevolent cycle evolves. People feel good seeing their ideas in action, which leads to more improvement ideas. You'll be impressed by what people come up with.

Kaizen Circle Activity

Kaizen circle activity[3] (KCA) is perhaps the best known involvement activity. It enjoyed a brief vogue during the 1980s as North American companies sought to imitate the Japanese success. But the soil was still infertile.

KCA confers great benefits:[4]

1. Strengthens team members' ability to:
   a. Work as part of a team.
   b. Lead a team.
   c. Think clearly and logically.
   d. Solve problems.
2. Builds team-member confidence. Team members feel good knowing they have contributed to the company's success. They are ready for the next challenge.
3. Attacks critical problems with "hundreds of hands."

Structure of KCA

A manager with a problem usually triggers a kaizen circle and acts as the sponsor. The circle usually comprises six to eight team members who meet for an hour or so, once a week for six to eight weeks.[5]

A circle usually culminates with a presentation to management on results achieved and future activity.

Figure 7.1[6] describes kaizen circle roles and responsibilities. Some roles are optional. For example, circle trainers may not be required for experienced circles. Often a single person, for example, an experienced area supervisor, can act as both facilitator and advisor.

KCA Training

To successfully conduct circles, team members must be trained in

- *Administrative skills*: How to hold team meetings, make assignments, take minutes, prepare presentations, and so on
- *Brainstorming*: How to generate ideas while involving all circle members
- *Problem solving*
- *Presentation skills*: How to present findings to management

At Toyota our KCA training is completed in four hours.

Role	Responsibilities
Circle Member	Attend meetings Contribute ideas Choose and analyze problem Recommend and implement solutions Make presentations
Facilitator	Attend training Guide team members through problem-solving process Attend circle meetings Complete and submit KCA meeting records
Advisor	Attend training Provide technical or administrative advice as required Attend circle meetings Help coordinate presentations to management
Circle Trainer	Develop and conduct training Attend circle meetings if requested Provide problem-solving training if requested Collect meeting records and report to management
Manager	Encourage circle formation and involvement Periodically check circle progress and offers suggestions Approve recommendations Attend presentations

Figure 7.1   Kaizen circle roles and responsibilities

KCA Administration

KCA requires a control department[7] to promote and administer it. The main administrative tasks are

- Creating standard forms to support circles
- Registering new circles
- Recording the results of each circle
- Reporting macro KCA results and trends
- Training

At Toyota Cambridge our human resources team served as the control department for all involvement activities. Figure 7.2[8] shows a generic kaizen circle report format.

Start Date: Target Completion Date:

Problem Identification	Circle Theme	Circle Topic

2. Circle Advisor: _____ 4. _____
  Circle Leader: _____ 5. _____
  Circle Members: 1. _____ 6. _____
              2. _____ 7. _____
              3. _____ 8. _____

Team Name:

3. Problem Selection	Problem Statement

Target

Activity Schedule

4. Root Cause Analysis

5. Countermeasure
    (Development & Implementation)

6. Countermeasure Verification

Figure 7.2 Kaizen circle activity (sample report format).

KCA Promotion

At Toyota we promoted KCA through

- Report boards in production areas and other high-traffic locations such as team member entrances. KCA boards should describe the KCA process and objectives and celebrate circle accomplishments.
- Plantwide circle competitions and awards in categories such as productivity, safety, quality, cost, and environment.
- Interplant circle competitions.

Interplant circle competitions held at the company's head office and judged by senior management are highly motivating, particularly for young workers.

Role of the Manager

At Toyota I came to see that the manager's support is the best KCA promotion.[9] This means daily communication with team members about the company's critical issues and problems in their area and about management's expectation of KCA around important themes. KCA themes should be simple to begin with, such as quality or safety. As team members become more adept, KCA can focus on specific company goals such as reducing a particular kind of quality defect or improving ergonomics in assembly operations.

In addition, managers must

- Consider how to increase KCA in their areas.
- Regularly check the themes, estimated date of completion, and status of each circle in their areas.
- Personally check with circle members. A simple "How is it going?" or "Any problems?" goes a long way.
- Actively support circles that are having trouble with ideas and offer advice to ensure each circle achieves something concrete.
- Personally view the results each circle achieves and personally thank each team member for his or her efforts.

HOW WILL YOU MOTIVATE PEOPLE, PASCAL-SAN?

An esteemed Toyota sensei asked me this many years ago. Being a young, somewhat thick engineer and manager, I failed to grasp the question's significance. My core mental models included: *Improvement entails smart people (just like me) developing cunning strategies and telling people what to do!*

I learned the hard way that plans are lifeless unless the team wants to implement them.

And why should they want to? Improvement is hard, and change hurts. By contrast, doing nothing is easy. So how does a leader motivate people to do extraordinary things?

Here's what I have found.

SAFETY AND SECURITY ARE JOB ONE

If people don't feel secure in their jobs, forget it. Safety first is the mantra at great companies—and that means both physical and psychological safety.

NOBLE GOALS

People want to be involved in something bigger than themselves. "No man is an island," said the poet John Donne. People will die for a noble idea, a just cause. Great leaders are storytellers who frame the challenge in a compelling narrative. Team members thereby feel they are "building a cathedral," and not simply "cutting stone" (more in Chapter 8).

SIMPLE DECENCY AND THE GREAT VIRTUES[10]

The great virtues are enduring standards of ethical behavior. In Chapter 3 we learned that standards are important in management because they make problems visible. The same is true of ethical standards. Simple decency and the great virtues allow people to relax, which unleashes their creativity.

Advances in brain imaging technology support these observations. Under stress, our prefrontal cortex (PFC), the brain's managerial center, shuts down. Our old, reptilian limbic brain starts firing, triggering fight or flight and other thoughtless responses. In other words, *fear makes us stupid.* Deming intuited this decades ago in one of his Fourteen Points: "Drive fear out of the organization!"

When we're relaxed, by contrast, the PFC lights up like a proverbial Christmas tree.

Safety, noble goals, and simple decency are simply good business. Great organizations, those that have prospered for generations, understand this in their marrow.

For more on the great virtues, please refer to *Reflections of a Business Nomad* by Pascal Dennis (Toronto: Skopelos Press, 2012).

Practical Kaizen Training

Practical kaizen training (PKT) is an intense weeklong activity whose objective is[11]

■ Team member and supervisor training
■ Improvement of a specific process

As with KCA, the trigger for a PKT is usually a manager with a problem.

An individual PKT comprises three to four team members. A PKT event usually includes several teams and PKT instructors or advisors. The week is divided as follows:[12]

- One and a half days training
- Three days on the shop floor
- A half day presenting results to management

PKT participants should make physical changes, if possible. Small tools training should be available, and workers who seek these skills should be encouraged to participate.

PKT training should address

- Muda
- Standardized work
- Kaizen

At Toyota our desired output for each PKT was usually confirmed standard work charts for the newly designed process, physical changes, and a shared understanding across shifts of the new process.

Key Factors for PKT Success

Communication

Communication with workers and supervisors of all shifts is essential for PKT success. This includes up-front discussion of the objectives of the PKT and a garnering of ideas from team members who do the work. Proposed changes to process and equipment must be confirmed with all shifts.

Grasping the Situation

PKT members must grasp what is actually happening. This means measuring actual cycle times, WIP, machine performance, and the like. They must compare what the worker is actually doing to the existing standard work chart. There are often discrepancies, which are clues to process problems.

Problem Solving

PKT members must be scientists rigorously confirming every action by using the PDCA cycle. All changes must be based on observation and measurement. At Toyota I came to understand a peculiar thing: we do not teach the scientific method well in school. Indeed, I have since realized that at Toyota the intimate understanding of the scientific method at each level is perhaps the company's greatest strength.[13]

Role of the Supervisor

There is a Toyota saying that "The supervisor is almighty." Indeed, the supervisor is arguably the key to Lean success.[14] His or her role is not only to produce the required quantity and quality, but also to lead kaizen.

Kaizen leadership has four levels:

■ Level 1. Tell the team member what to do.
■ Level 2. Show the team member how it is done.
■ Level 3. Do it with the team member.
■ Level 4. Let the team member do it for himself and spur learning by asking questions.

Knowing how to ask questions is an important skill. A Lean sensei rarely tells the team member the answer. Rather, she guides the student toward self-discovery.

Suggestion Programs

Effective suggestion programs directly channel team member ideas to management and reward team member initiative. At Toyota I was amazed at the amount of effort expended in promoting team-member suggestions. I came to understand that the overriding goal was to engage each person—a thousand eyes, a thousand hands—in improvement.

Successful suggestion programs share the following characteristics:

■ Hassle-free process.
■ Quick decision-making and feedback to the team member.
■ Fairness. No one group should have unfair access to rewards.

- Promotion.
- Rewards for both extrinsic and intrinsic motivation.

Hassle-Free Process and Clear Rules

Suggestion program rules should be clear and simple, as should standards for turnaround time and rewards. Over time we developed a simple formula for calculating the value of a suggestion. An effective approach is to award benefit points per suggestion. Team members could cash out benefit points as they accrued. Gift vouchers may also be provided in lieu of cash. Suggestion forms should be one-page long and cover the following information:

- Source information (e.g., suggester, department, date, and similar identifying information)
- Suggestion topic (e.g., safety, quality, cost control, productivity, space, and environment)
- Current situation
- Suggested changes (kaizens)
- Results of kaizen
- Data supporting results

Supervisors should help their team members complete and submit suggestions. Program rules and standards should be summarized on the back of the form and should cover tangible and intangible suggestions.[15]

Tangible Suggestions

These are suggestions that result in documented savings in dollars, space, time (labor), or other measurable units. Here are common areas in which tangible benefits are found:

- *Cost savings:* Less material or energy used
- *Nonlabor savings:* Reduced transport costs, reduced packaging
- *Labor:* Reduced downtime or repair time
- *Ergonomic burden:* Reduced work burden[16]
- *Space:* Floor space saved

Intangible Suggestions

These are suggestions that generate identifiable improvements that produce no direct dollar, time, or space savings. Examples include

- *Safety:* Elimination of a hazard
- *Quality:* Prevention of a defect
- *5S:* Reduced hassle
- *Environmental:* Potential for spill eliminated

Quick Decision-Making and Feedback

A firm standard should be applied to feedback, such as, "We will respond to all suggestions within one week." A clear process and standards support quick turnaround. The evaluator's role is also critical.

Evaluators assess suggestions and recommend recognition levels. There should be enough evaluators in each department to meet the turnaround standards. Evaluators should be recognized for their work. At Toyota we invited evaluators to suggestion program dinners, where we presented the "Evaluator of the Year" award.

Fairness

I have found that some groups such as maintenance may have unfair access to suggestion program benefits. This creates resentment that could affect the prestige of the program. We strove to develop rules that would level the playing field.

Promotion

Suggestion programs should be promoted through

- Report boards, both on the shop floor and in team-member entrances
- Dinners where outstanding suggestions and evaluators can be recognized
- Regular reporting and feedback to management of process and outcome results

Measurement always works. Relevant measures include

- Total number of suggestions

- Suggestions per team member
- Supervisor participation percentage
- Approval ratio
- Points awarded
- Average points per team member
- Percentage of intangible suggestions

However, at Toyota we learned not to overemphasize these numbers. For example, we avoided setting annual number targets. Otherwise, we found that some area supervisors might pester team members for suggestions at month end merely to achieve quotas. Rather, we let numbers grow naturally.

Extrinsic and Intrinsic Motivation

Extrinsic motivators include cash and gifts and are the most common rewards of suggestion programs. But they may not be the most powerful motivators. The psychological literature indicates that intrinsic motivators such as the following may be more important:

- Recognition by peers
- Contribution to a broader goal or value such as environment or safety
- Development of leadership and other skills
- Personal growth and self-actualization

My personal experience confirms the power of internal motivators. However, I have also found that cash and gift rewards have their place.

How to Motivate Suggestions

The organization's culture is the soil in which all involvement activities grow. Management must create a nurturing soil by living values such as

- Openness
- Mutual trust
- Teamwork
- Customer focus
- Training

At Toyota we developed an annual culture *hoshin* (plan)[17] to strengthen these values.

This is more difficult in a brownfield plant. I recall a veteran worker saying to me, "I've been here for 30 years. This is the first time anyone has asked for my opinion." The culture hoshin must be even better in a brownfield plant.

Area supervisors and managers are responsible for motivating involvement by their team members. Here are some concrete activities that they can support:

- "What bugs me" boards, also known as suggestion seed boards, in work areas. These comprise a simple matrix with the following headings: problem, possible countermeasures, next step, and result.
- Seed books in team-member meeting areas.
- Team brainstorming sessions focusing on the biggest problems of the department and company.

Monthly or quarterly themes can also be helpful. One of our most effective quarterly themes at Toyota was "Ergonomics—the right moves in the workplace." We received and implemented hundreds of excellent ideas that reduced strain for our team members. Environmental themes are proved effective. One suggestion triggered a plantwide recycling system that continues today.

Quantity First—Then Quality

The rule of thumb in any suggestion program is "quantity first, then quality." It usually takes three to five years for a suggestion program to generate good quantity (e.g., five to ten suggestions per team member per year). When we have achieved volume, then we can focus on quality.[18]

Annual Culture Hoshin

There should be an annual company culture hoshin that sets goals for KCA, PKT, and suggestions. KCA targets might include

- *KCA outcome targets:* The number of circles completed, the number of successful kaizens, and dollars saved

■ *KCA process targets*: The number of team members participating, number of team members trained, quality of circles, quality of KCA training, and satisfaction of team members with KCA

Involvement has to be managed.

Summary

Team member involvement is the heart of Lean production. Involvement develops the capability of our team members and improves our prospects for long-term success. I have described kaizen circle activity, practical kaizen training, and suggestion programs. Supervisors and managers play the key role in sustaining involvement. Involvement activities must be fair, hassle-free systems, and should satisfy both extrinsic and intrinsic motivators. There should be an annual culture hoshin to support and sustain involvement. Involvement should be managed as adroitly as production or quality.

Endnotes

1. Discussion with Toyota executive.
2. Henry Mintzberg, *Managers Not MBAs* (Berrett Koehler, San Francisco 2004).
3. Also known as small-group activity.
4. Discussion with Toyota executive.
5. Toyota training document.
6. Ibid.
7. The control department concept is discussed in detail in Chapter 8.
8. Toyota training document.
9. Discussion with Toyota executive.
10. Pascal Dennis, *Reflections of a Business Nomad* (Skopelos Press, Toronto 2012).
11. Discussion with Toyota executive.
12. Toyota training document.
13. Steven Spear and H. Kent Bowen, "Decoding the DNA of the Toyota Production System," *Harvard Business Review* (Sept.–Oct. 1999).
14. Discussion with Toyota executive.
15. Discussion with Toyota executive.
16. To quantify these benefits a simple ergonomic burden measuring system would be required.
17. Hoshin planning is discussed further in Chapter 8.
18. Discussion with Toyota executive.

Study Questions

1. Describe at least three formal methods through which your organization involves frontline team members.
   a. What are the strengths and weaknesses of these methods of involvement?
   b. How might your organization improve each activity?
2. In your experience, what are the biggest obstacles to total involvement?
   a. What are possible countermeasures?
3. What are the relative strengths and weaknesses of Quick & Easy kaizen, suggestion programs, kaizen circle activity, and practical kaizen training?
4. Describe a Quick & Easy kaizen process with which you're familiar.
   a. What makes it effective (or ineffective)?
   b. How might you improve the process?
5. Describe a kaizen circle process with which you're familiar.
   a. What makes it effective (or ineffective)?
   b. How might you improve the process?
6. How do you motivate people to become involved in improvement?

Chapter 8

Hoshin Planning

Step by step, walk the thousand-mile road.

Miyamoto Musashi[1]

Knowledge waste is perhaps the most pervasive waste. Indeed, if the popularity of Dilbert is any indication, knowledge waste is at epidemic proportions in North America. According to Thomas Homer-Dixon,[2] we are struggling with an ingenuity gap: a shortfall between our rapidly rising need for ingenuity and our inadequate supply. Homer-Dixon argues that there are two kinds of ingenuity: technical and social. We have the former in abundance. The constraint is not technology but governance.

We require a social ingenuity to answer questions such as

- How do we identify our critical goals?
- How do we develop plans and align our activities?
- How do we communicate our goals' activities level by level?
- How do we harness the abundant talent of our team members?
- How do we sustain our activities?
- How do we quickly change course when required?
- How do we learn from our experience?

Toyota has developed effective answers to many of these questions, which we examine in this chapter and the next one.

What Is Planning?

Despite graduate-level training in business and engineering, I did not learn how to plan until I got to Toyota. I had learned technical ingenuity but it was not enough. Thomas Homer-Dixon has pointed out that our current ingenuity gap involves social ingenuity.

Planning means answering two questions:

- Where are we going?
- How do we get there?

There are four kinds of planning in the modern organization:

- *Operational*: How will we manage day to day?
- *Financial*: How will we spend our budget?
- *Project*: How will we achieve this specific goal?
- *Strategic*: Where are we going and how do we get there?

In this chapter we focus on strategic planning.

The road metaphor shown in Figure 8.1[3] frames our discussion. To plan effectively, we need to understand

- Where we are
- Where we are going (vision)
- How we will get there (plan)
- What boulders and small stones are on the path

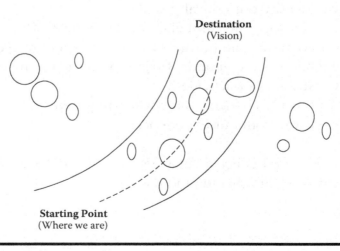

Figure 8.1   The road metaphor.

We must also be careful not to be diverted by boulders that are off the path.

Why Plan?

We plan to develop a shared vision of where we are going and how we will get there. Indeed, at Toyota I came to realize that planning itself should be a pull system: our vision so compelling that it pulls us into the future.

But we also plan for less obvious reasons:

- To improve as individuals and as an organization
- To compel renewal and reinvention
- To learn

Effective planning compels us to take stock of our strengths and weaknesses and to take countermeasures. Planning also bursts the bubble of complacency by continually setting breakthrough goals. We can never sit on our laurels.

Finally, Peter Senge's concept of the "learning organization"[4] is much quoted but perhaps not well understood. The concept has no meaning unless there are management systems that record and share important learning points. Moreover, the concept is ineffectual unless our planning system recognizes and applies the learning.

Problems with Planning

Strategic planning is every manager's unfavorite activity.

Henry Mintzberg

Mintzberg was only half-joking. Indeed, his classic, *The Rise and Fall of Strategic Planning*, describes in often painful detail the weaknesses of conventional planning. There is an embarrassment of riches, as it were. Here are but a few:

- Unrealistic forecasts or expectations; the planning process is too rigid to adapt to changing conditions.
- Goals are set arbitrarily with no clear link to need, means, or feasibility.
- Too many goals; inadequate focus.

- Wrong goals.
- Goals are not SMART.[5]
- Planned activities are not regularly reviewed; disconnect in time.
- Planned activities are reviewed punitively.
- Planning is regarded as an event, rather than as an ongoing process.
- Planning is done in the absence of data.
- Data is overanalyzed.
- A separate department does planning.
- Inadequate communication between and within departments; horizontal and vertical alignment disconnect.
- Management team is reluctant to take stock of strengths and weaknesses.

Planning problems, in summary, are largely caused by disconnects:

- Horizontal (within departments)
- Vertical (between departments)
- Temporal (in time)

These in turn create the terrible waste of knowledge. In fact, there are nine types of knowledge waste. The corresponding symbols are shown in Figure 8.2.[6]

How Do We Create Flow?

Most organizations have an abundance of energy and talent. Yet we struggle to achieve our goals. We seek to create flow of knowledge, experience, and creativity in our organization. We seek to involve all levels and bring creative talent to bear on our critical strategic problems. But how?

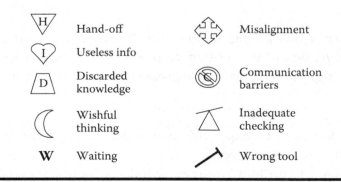

Figure 8.2 The nine wastes of knowledge.

Hoshin Planning[7]

Hoshin kanri means[8]

- Shining metal or compass
- Ship in a storm on the right path
- Strategic policy deployment

Hoshin kanri or hoshin planning is the nervous system of Lean production. Hoshin[9] planning is the short-term (one year) and long-term (three-to five-year) process used to identify and address critical business needs and develop the capability of our people, achieved by aligning company resources at all levels and applying the PDCA cycle to consistently achieve critical results.

Focus of Hoshin Planning

Hoshin planning targets the critical few problems, the big boulders on our road (Figure 8.3), which are the key to improvement. Our operational plan handles the small stones, that is, the routine work. A common mistake is to take on too much, dilute energy thereby, and achieve nothing in the end.

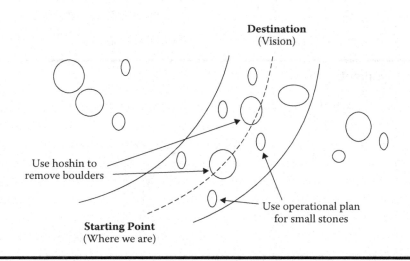

Figure 8.3   The road metaphor with problems targeted.

ROUTINE WORK AND IMPROVEMENT WORK

Managerial work has two parts: routine work and improvement work. The formal organizational structure is good at the former, but not so good at the latter, because improvement work requires cross-functionality. Moreover, many managers believe their job has no relation to improvement and make no space for it in their daily work. Others would like to make space for improvement work but are overwhelmed by the crises of the day.

Hoshin planning keeps improvement work on the radar screen. Our mother A3 strategies and control departments provide the cross-functional structure improvement work requires. Without improvement work, we'll keep getting the results we've always gotten.

Alignment and Flexibility

Through hoshin planning we seek to align our resources (Figure 8.4) and to quickly identify and respond to changes in the business environment (Figure 8.5).

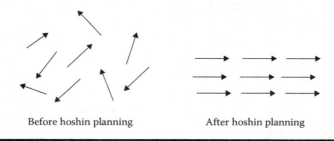

Before hoshin planning   After hoshin planning

Figure 8.4   Alignment.

As the business environment changes, company activities must change quickly.

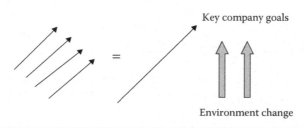

Key company goals

Environment change

Figure 8.5   Flexibility.

POINT, FLOW, AND SYSTEM IMPROVEMENT

Leaders are responsible for leading improvement, commensurate with their scope and span of control. It makes little sense for a frontline team leader to hunt the great white whale of system kaizen. Similarly, it's suboptimal for a senior vice-president to focus her attention solely on point kaizen, when she should be looking for Moby Dick.

Here are some working definitions of point, flow, and system improvement.

POINT IMPROVEMENT

This entails improving a point in the value stream, for example:

■ Machine changeover
■ Material handling
■ Quality (e.g., damage to packaging, contamination)
■ Ergonomics
■ Standardized work: Lack of; wrong content/sequence/timing, and so on

FLOW IMPROVEMENT

This entails several point kaizens that add up to an overall value stream improvement (e.g., lead time, throughput, or inventory turns).

Image: A + B + C + D = overall VS improvement, where A, B, C, and D might be improvements in

■ Machine changeover
■ Material handling
■ Quality (e.g., damage to packaging, contamination)
■ Ergonomics
■ Standardized work (e.g., wrong content, sequence, and/or timing)

SYSTEM IMPROVEMENT

This entails continuing to ask why until we uncover systemic causes to recurrent problems. Typically system kaizen focuses on man/woman, machine, methods, or materials systems, or core business processes such as budgeting, forecasting, and information systems.

Hoshin Planning and MBO

Hoshin planning is the logical enhancement to management by objectives (MBO) introduced by Peter Drucker in his 1954 classic, *The Practice of Management*.[10] Hoshin planning builds on the strengths of MBO and avoids its weaknesses.[11]

Drucker deeply influenced Japanese management thinking. Companies including Toyota developed hoshin planning by refining Drucker's ideas. Important enhancements include

■ Focus on objectives and process
■ PDCA and metrics
■ Nemawashi
■ Catchball
■ People focus

These are discussed in detail in the following sections.

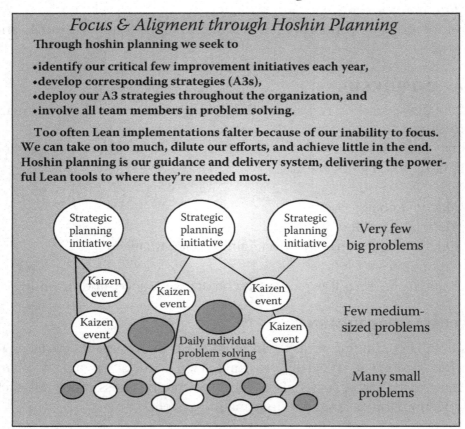

Focus & Aligment through Hoshin Planning

Through hoshin planning we seek to

•**identify our critical few improvement initiatives each year,**
•**develop corresponding strategies (A3s),**
•**deploy our A3 strategies throughout the organization, and**
•**involve all team members in problem solving.**

Too often Lean implementations falter because of our inability to focus. We can take on too much, dilute our efforts, and achieve little in the end. Hoshin planning is our guidance and delivery system, delivering the powerful Lean tools to where they're needed most.

Strategic planning initiative

Very few big problems

Kaizen event

Daily individual problem solving

Few medium-sized problems

Many small problems

Hoshin Planning System

The hoshin planning system comprises the following:

- Plan-do-check-act
- Nemawashi
- Catchball
- Control department concept
- A3 thinking

PDCA

Hoshin planning comprises overlapping PDCA cycles (Figure 8.6):[12]

- *Macro (three to five years):* Practiced by senior management
- *Annual:* Practiced by operating managers
- *Micro (weekly, monthly, and biannual):* Practiced by operating managers and their subordinates

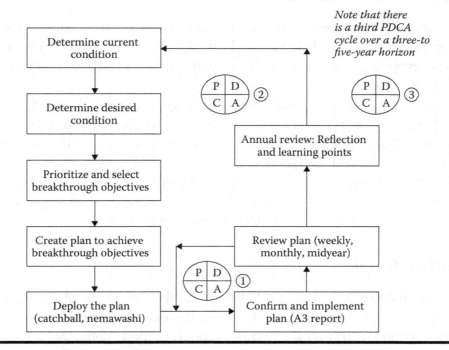

Figure 8.6   Hoshin planning process.

PDCA requires supportive management systems that make the current status visible to all and that compel countermeasures. These can include both formal and informal reviews.

Formal reviews should be held every six months (at the beginning of the year, midyear, and at year end). The year-end review entails a summary of what happened and informs next year's strategic plan (which is presented in January). Less formal reviews can include

- Daily status reports shared by the management team
- Weekly management team meetings wherein department heads report status
- Shop floor process reviews of hot items

PDCA also requires a solid understanding of metrics and visual management. SMART goals must be developed both for outcomes and the process. Control panels or dashboards need to be generated on a daily basis with minimal effort. Visual systems such as report boards and line-side process reviews help to create shared understanding of the data.

Check Outcomes and Process

MBO tends to emphasize outcomes instead of means. The leader's message to subordinates often is, "I don't care how you do it, just do it."[13] This causes stress and erodes morale. The leader is also saying, "I don't care about you or your problems."

Subordinates, bitterly remembering their own experiences, often perpetuate this behavior when they become leaders. "Why should you have it any better than I did?" This also hinders learning, which requires that we understand why we achieved, or failed to achieve, our objectives.

By contrast, hoshin planning requires leaders to engage their subordinates on the means as well as the ends. Leaders are expected to guide their teams based on their deeper knowledge and experience.

Strengthen People

Leaders must also ask, "How can I strengthen the capability of my people?" If we fail to achieve a goal, instead of blaming people, we should ask why five times. Then we should make a plan to strengthen them. Only a poor leader puts people in situations they are incapable of handling.

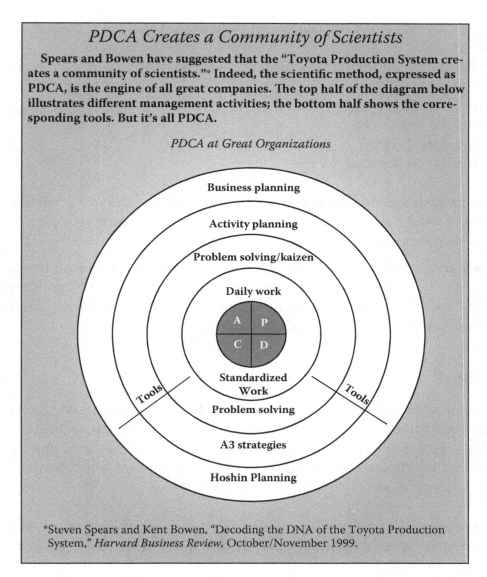

PDCA Creates a Community of Scientists

Spears and Bowen have suggested that the "Toyota Production System creates a community of scientists."* Indeed, the scientific method, expressed as PDCA, is the engine of all great companies. The top half of the diagram below illustrates different management activities; the bottom half shows the corresponding tools. But it's all PDCA.

PDCA at Great Organizations

Business planning

Activity planning

Problem solving/kaizen

Daily work

A | P

C | D

Standardized Work

Tools   Tools

Problem solving

A3 strategies

Hoshin Planning

*Steven Spears and Kent Bowen, "Decoding the DNA of the Toyota Production System," Harvard Business Review, October/November 1999.

By contrast, a good leader gauges team member capability and gives assignments that are just beyond them. This helps to strengthen each person. Team members appreciate the leader's concern for their development. This too helps to create alignment.

Nemawashi

This elegant word means "to prepare a tree for transplanting" and connotes the process of consensus building that creates alignment.[14] Nemawashi entails reviewing a hoshin with all affected customers before its implementation.

Planning, therefore, usually takes longer, but implementation is quicker and more effective.

Who are the customers of a hoshin? Those who will

■ Execute the plan
■ Be affected by the plan
■ Approve the plan
■ Be able to improve the plan

Nemawashi involves numerous revisions based on customer feedback. But there will be no unpleasant surprises when you present your plan to senior management.

A Caveat: Consensus building does not mean that I must give up my ideas or beliefs. Nor does it mean that we must all agree before a hoshin is implemented. At times we may agree to disagree. But consensus does mean that I will support the decision of the group.

Catchball

Catchball refers to the give and take required between and among management levels during the planning process.[15] Through catchball, strategies and tactics[16] cascade through the organization. The catchball seeks to link the vision of the officers and the daily activities of shop floor team members. Here is how it works:

1. Company officers develop a vision of what the organization needs to do, and capabilities that need to be developed. They "toss" the vision to senior managers.
2. Senior managers "catch" the officers' vision and translate it into hoshins. Then they toss them back to the officers, and ask, in effect, "Is this what you mean? Will these activities achieve our vision?"
3. Officers provide feedback and guidance to senior managers. The hoshins can be passed back and forth several times.
4. Eventually a consensus is reached. Officers and senior managers agree that, "These are the hoshins that our company will use to achieve our vision."
5. Senior managers now toss their hoshins to middle managers, who catch them and translate them into activities. These in turn are

tossed back to senior managers who provide feedback and guidance. Eventually, a consensus is reached. Senior and middle managers agree that, "These are the activities (hoshins) we will use to achieve the senior managers' hoshins, which in turn will achieve our company vision."

6. Middle managers will in turn toss their hoshins to their subordinates.

The process culminates with the performance objectives of individual team members.

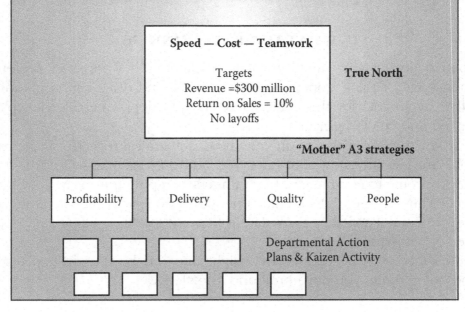

The Planning and Execution Tree

The outcome of hoshin planning is a tree of activities with True North—our strategic and philosophical goal at the top. True North comprises our hard business goals, normally financial measures, and our broad-brush goal—a short phrase expressing our vision, direction, and values. The broad-brush goal is not simply a marketing slogan. We need to arrive at these few words viscerally, through deeply felt emotion and experience.

Our business fundamentals or focus areas comprise the second level of the tree, and we develop a so-called "mother" A3 for each of them. Toyota's hoshin planning focus areas are Safety, Quality, Delivery, and Cost. But these may not be right for your organization. Business fundamentals for a health care, financial services, or retail organization might differ from those of a manufacturer. The important thing is to think it through and chart your own course.

The third level of the tree is departmental action plans and kaizen activity, which are derived through the catchball process. Departmental action plans are sometimes called "baby" A3s. Here is a sample planning and execution tree.

Speed — Cost — Teamwork

Targets
Revenue =$300 million
Return on Sales = 10%
No layoffs

True North

"Mother" A3 strategies

| Profitability | Delivery | Quality | People |

Departmental Action
Plans & Kaizen Activity

The Control Department[17] Concept

At Toyota I came to understand that the control department concept was the key to breaking down the silos that cripple so many organizations.[18] Core company focus areas such as productivity, quality, cost, and safety require the coordinated effort of many groups. These are cross-functional goals. For example, to meet quality objectives, the following groups must pull together:

■ Manufacturing
■ Purchasing
■ Production control
■ Engineering
■ Maintenance
■ Quality

The control department, in this case quality, would coordinate the cross-functional activities required to achieve company goals. This includes

■ Leading the hoshin planning process for quality
■ Leading the setting of goals and means (through nemawashi and catchball)
■ Applying PDCA at the micro and annual level to confirm success
■ Making problems visible and supporting countermeasure activity

WHAT IS A KEY THINKER?

Control departments are our "key thinkers." They develop profound knowledge of their "zone," make diagnoses, and drive action planning. Other synonyms for this critical role include deployment leader, pacemaker, and chief engineer.

A key thinker is akin to an enzyme in a chemical reaction. Some reactions are glacially slow. But once you add the enzyme—whoosh—they quickly come to completion. Key thinkers "wrap their arms around" their zone. They go see, reflect, talk to people at all levels, and thereby grasp the situation. Then they formulate a hypothesis: "If we do A, B, and C, then X will happen."

Testable hypotheses give us insight into our business. Keep testing and before long, you have profound knowledge.

The best known key thinker is perhaps Toyota's famous "heavyweight chief engineer" or *shusa*. Famously, the shusa has few direct reports but is the most powerful person in the platform!

What makes for an effective key thinker?

■ Profound knowledge, passionate about his or her zone
■ Impatient with the status quo
■ Ornery, yet able to forge a consensus

They're a critical enabler in hoshin planning, and an important implementation question is, "How will we develop strong key thinkers?"

There are a number of subtleties here:

■ The control department develops the overall hoshin for the company. Individual departments support it with their own hoshins. For example, the quality department would develop the overall hoshin for the company. Each department would develop individual hoshins supporting the company hoshin.
■ The control department is responsible for the trends; the line departments are responsible for the annual result. Line departments have authority and must accept responsibility. Thus, the manufacturing department is responsible for its own quality results. But the quality department is responsible for highlighting a deteriorating trend and working with the manufacturing department to solve it.

PUT YOUR STRATEGY ON A DIET

More companies die from over-eating than from starvation.

Dave Packard

Slimming down our strategy is often our biggest challenge. "Just one more..." seems to be a compulsion in many organizations. (I often joke about the "critical few hundred.") This usually results in obese lumbering strategies with little hope of success. Worst of all, we alienate our team members. As leaders add more and more to the pile, team members grimace and think, "You pretend to give us a reasonable strategy, and we'll pretend to do it."

Why do otherwise capable leaders behave this way?

In part, they're trying to buffer uncertainty. "We don't really know what's happening, so we'll keep pressing buttons. Something is bound to work!" Surely, a better approach is to take the time to grasp the situation, before developing plans!

A second cause is an all-too-common mental model: "If I jam the pipeline full of stuff, more will come out the other end!" This, of course, contravenes the laws of production physics (see Chapter 5). The pipeline turns to cement and nothing flows. Unsophisticated leaders may then resort to exhortation (or worse). Which is akin to asking your team members to jump out the window, and after they crash, telling them, "Flap your arms faster!"

How do we avoid all this?

The most important word in hoshin planning is *No*. Most organizations need to put their strategy on a diet. Less is more. In practice, this means a rigorous screening process. Nothing gets into the "hoshin hopper" unless it meets stringent criteria, such as

- The purpose of the activity has been clearly defined and explicitly linked to our strategic vision and objectives.
- There is a clear problem statement and a sound strategy (A3).
- Root causes are clearly identified.
- Hypothesis has been articulated. "If we do this, then I believe that will happen."
- Actions address most important root causes.
- Reasonable cost–benefit analysis has been done.

Remember, the most important word in hoshin planning is *No*.[19]

A3 Thinking

An A3 report is a one-page story on 11" × 17" paper.[20,21] A3s were originally used at Toyota in the 1960s to summarize kaizen circle activities. They have perhaps become Toyota's most effective communication tools. There are now four kinds of A3s:

- *Hoshin planning A3:* Used to summarize department and company hoshins
- *Problem solving A3:* Used to summarize problems and countermeasures
- *Proposal A3:* Used to present new ideas
- *Current status A3:* Used to summarize current condition of a hoshin, problem, or concern

Over time, I began to understand that A3 was a way of thinking rooted in PDCA, nemawashi, and catchball. A good A3 reflects a sound grasp of the situation and mastery of core Lean tools and thinking. But the piece of paper is less important than the process.

History of Report Writing

Report writing has developed over the past century in support of the modern organization. Different formats have been used, including

- Discussion papers
- Issues notes
- Dissertations

Common Report-Writing Problems

A major problem is no standard. Report formats often vary from department to department, or even from section to section. Imagine an economy in which everyone uses a different currency. How effective would economic transactions be?

A second problem is bulk, or the "better by the pound" syndrome. How often have you been handed a strategic plan that is several inches thick? Did you bother to read it? Even executive summaries are 10 or 20 pages long. Reading such stuff will kill your quality of life.

Figure 8.7[22] shows the format of the hoshin planning A3. It is essentially a storyboard following a logical and standard structure. The structure can be modified to show current status or to address problems as they arise. Figure 8.8[23] shows the format for a current status A3 that could be used to report hoshin progress.

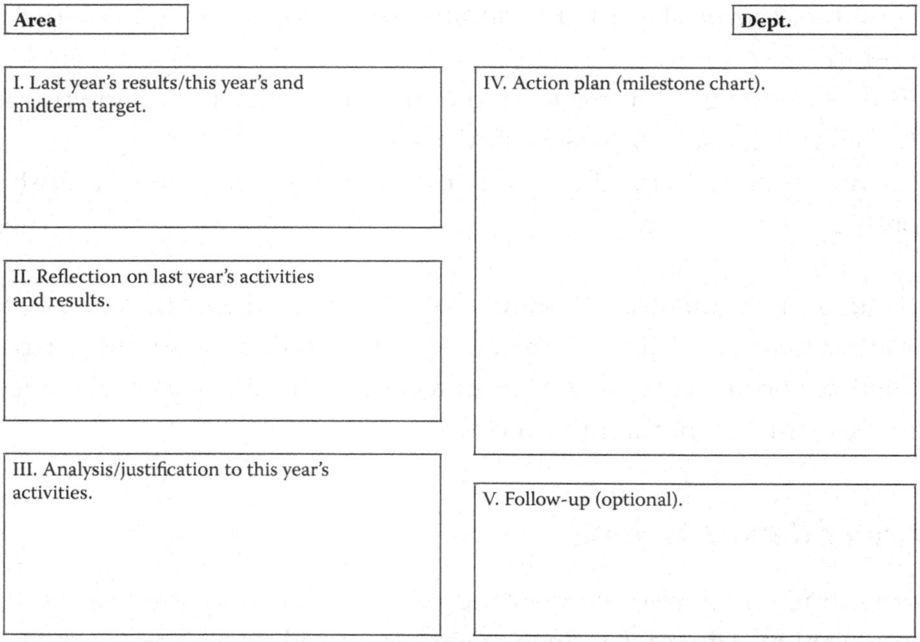

Area		Dept.

I. Last year's results/this year's and midterm target.	IV. Action plan (milestone chart).
II. Reflection on last year's activities and results.	
III. Analysis/justification to this year's activities.	V. Follow-up (optional).

Figure 8.7   Strategic planning A3.

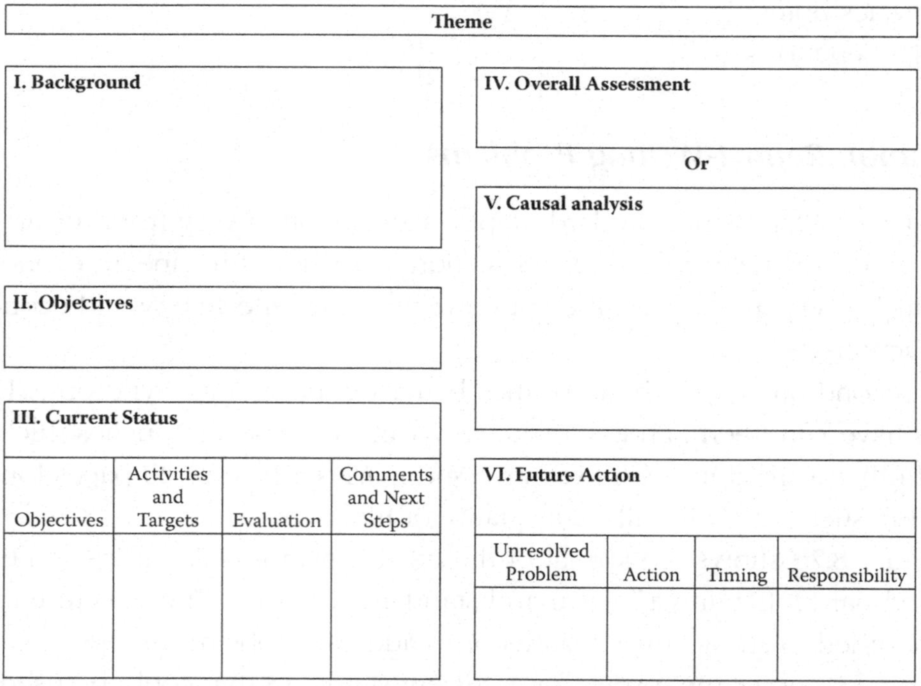

Theme

I. Background	IV. Overall Assessment
	Or
	V. Causal analysis
II. Objectives	
III. Current Status	VI. Future Action

Objectives	Activities and Targets	Evaluation	Comments and Next Steps

Unresolved Problem	Action	Timing	Responsibility

Figure 8.8   Current status A3.

Telling Stories with A3s

Initially, A3s may seem "too complicated" or "too busy"—a normal reaction to a thorough A3. We're condensing a great deal into a small space. But you'll find that A3 stories have an intuitive flow and can be told in less than ten minutes. The author tells the story; we follow along, and then have a question and answer session.

By the time the A3 is presented to senior management, everybody in the room has already seen and commented on it. At Toyota I found that it wasn't unusual for an immediate decision to be made after a ten-minute presentation.

A3 Logical Flow

Strategy A3 Theme	
What strategic objectives do we need to achieve this year? How did we do last year? What's our history?	What's our action plan to achieve these objectives? (Who, what, when, where, and how)
What did we do last year? What activities worked? Why? What didn't work? Why? What have we learned?	
What do we need to do to achieve this year's strategic objectives? What's our rationale, our story?	Anything bothering you? Do you need any help with anything? Any unresolved issues?

There are dangers though. A3s can be appealing to people short of time and overwhelmed with paper and electronic reports. One piece of paper looks good, and the A3 becomes a dictate from management, a shiny new toy that everyone must use. "From now on, everything will be A3!"

Or people can try to outdo one another by creating fancy graphics, or by condensing more and more information on the page. Please remember the purpose of A3s: to gain a shared understanding of an important issue, so we can solve problems, and get results.

THE IMPORTANCE OF LANGUAGE

"In the beginning was the Word." Language reflects how we think, how we experience life, and who we are. Strategy is storytelling; strategy is language. A common failure mode is foggy confusing language. For example, what's a team to make of head-scratchers like the following?

> "We will leverage our World Class Operating Capabilities," or "We'll reshape pricing tactics to effectively manage demand while sustaining market access."
>
> Such language is alienating.
>
> Let's use plain language instead. Ban jargon, clichés, and the latest buzzwords. Sayonara to "leverage," "synergy," "disintermediation," and "robust," to pick just a few.
>
> We were lucky at our old Toyota plant. Our Japanese senseis' grasp of English was very basic, which meant we had to express ourselves as simply and clearly as possible. As a result, we communicated beautifully.

The Four Phases of Hoshin Planning

Hoshin planning has four phases:[24]

- Hoshin generation
- Hoshin deployment
- Hoshin implementation
- Final evaluation

Each of these is discussed in the following sections.

Hoshin Generation

This means setting the annual goals of a company and its departments. Goals address both processes and outcomes and are usually developed by senior management in consultation with their subordinates. Here is an example for a quality department.

Company quality goal and means: We will reduce overall defect rates by 20% by year-end by

- Working with our key suppliers to correct our top 10 quality concerns
- Improving the capability of the three most important processes in each department
- Strengthening the involvement of our shop floor team members

These statements will be based on several iterations of catchball and nemawashi.

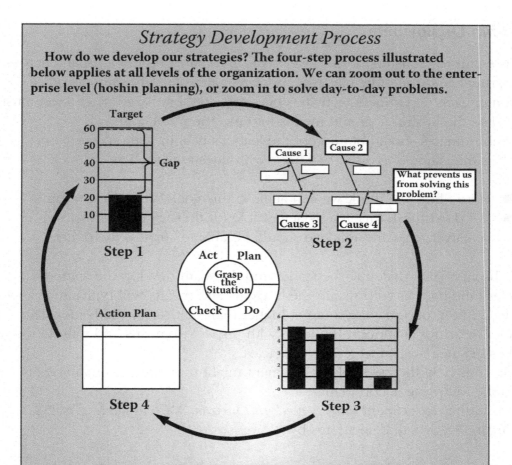

Strategy Development Process

How do we develop our strategies? The four-step process illustrated below applies at all levels of the organization. We can zoom out to the enterprise level (hoshin planning), or zoom in to solve day-to-day problems.

Step 1 entails defining the gap. For mother A3s the gap is normally an enterprise measure like revenue, profit, customer delivery and quality rates, and lost time injury rate. Step 2 entails asking, what prevents us?, and brainstorming using a fishbone diagram. Step 3 entails prioritizing possible causes in a Pareto chart.* Step 4 means developing our action plan (hypothesis) and expressing it on our A3.

The most common failure mode is jumping from step 1 to step 4. Here are other common failures:

- Not defining the gap; initiating activity without understanding what you're trying to improve, or by how much
- Superficial causal analysis
- Not prioritizing causes, or prioritizing without data
- Actions don't address the most important causes

It's hard work and there is no substitute for practice.

*Fishbone diagrams, also known as Cause and Effect diagrams, help to identify the causes of a problem or gap. Pareto charts prioritize causes in a bar chart. For more information, see Michael Brassard and Diane Ritter, *The Memory Jogger II, A Pocket Guide to Tools for Continuous Improvement and Effective Planning,* (Methuen MA: Goal/QPC, 1994).

Hoshin Deployment

This entails establishing lower-level goals and plans, both within and across departments, through nemawashi and catchball. As the hoshin cascades through each department, activities become more bite-sized. Each level must translate the hoshin goal and means into meaningful action.

Subordinates should not accept the leader's hoshin without question. Rather, they should toss the ball back with questions such as

- "Here's how we think we can achieve this goal. What do you think?"
- "We don't think this goal is achievable for these reasons. However, if we can do this and this, we should be able to surpass the target."

Through such dialogue the leader and the team develop the shared understanding that will sustain them. Goals and means will typically change. Indeed, the group may set a target higher than that set by the leader. The leader in turn will support the team with respect to means and will do the necessary nemawashi to reduce obstacles.

Here is how the assembly department might translate the quality goals into the following action plans.

Assembly department quality goal and means: We will achieve a 25%[25] reduction in overall defect rates by

- Setting up a task force on our top five quality concerns. The task force will include engineering, maintenance, and supplier representatives. Targets: Interim report—April 30; Final report—September 30.
- Implementing the process quality assurance activity across our department. Target: June 30.
- Strengthening team member involvement by putting all assembly team members through kaizen circle training. Target: Two kaizen circles on quality per supervisor per year.

Output of Hoshin Deployment

The output of hoshin deployment includes affinity and tree diagrams and A3 strategic plans. These are developed level by level through brainstorming sessions. In my consulting work, I typically spend a couple of days with each level starting with senior management. During the first year of hoshin planning it takes about two weeks per level to confirm alignment and to develop a shared strategy in the A3 format. After the second year the process develops roots and can be completed much more quickly.

Figures 8.9 and 8.10 show an affinity and tree diagram for the goal of "Winning the Stanley Cup." To stimulate brainstorming it is sometimes helpful to imagine that we have already achieved the goal and to ask, "How did we do it?"

Figure 8.9 Affinity diagram sample.

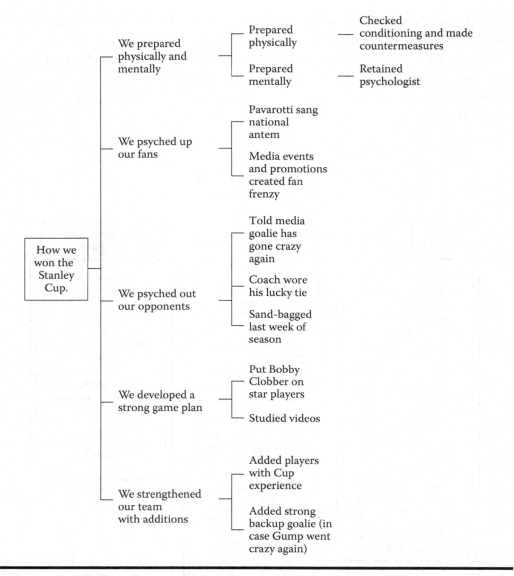

Figure 8.10 Tree diagram sample.

Note that our tree diagram has only five branches. A good rule of thumb is, "Have no more activities that you can count on the fingers of one hand." As noted, a common mistake is to take on too much. Pick a few boulders each year.

Figure 8.11 shows what a professional hockey team's annual strategic plan might look like.[26] Our plan should tell a coherent "story." Each section should naturally flow into the next.

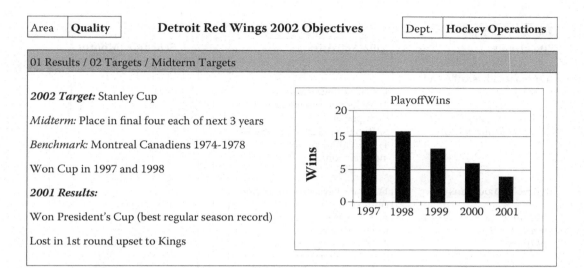

| Area | Quality | **Detroit Red Wings 2002 Objectives** | Dept. | **Hockey Operations** |

01 Results / 02 Targets / Midterm Targets

2002 Target: Stanley Cup

Midterm: Place in final four each of next 3 years

Benchmark: Montreal Canadiens 1974-1978

Won Cup in 1997 and 1998

2001 Results:

Won President's Cup (best regular season record)

Lost in 1st round upset to Kings

PlayoffWins

Reflection on '01 Activities

Activity	Rating	Key Results/Issues
Acquired free agent scorers to strengthen offense	G	Robitaille, Larionov had career years
Implemented high-speed attacking system	Y	Won President's Cup; Upset 1st playoff round
Strengthened special teams	G	Power play & penalty killing were best in NHL
Failed to find reliable backup goalie	R	Weak goaltending key factor in loss to Kings
Did not prepare adequately for Kings; focuses on Colorado, St. Louis & Dallas	R	Unprepared for Kings

Analysis/Justification to This Year's Activities

1) Regular season is basic preparation for playoffs. President's Cup is irrelevant.

2) Playoff hockey is defensive. High scoring teams vulnerable to obstruction & traps

3) In 2001 we were unprepared physically & psychologically. We took the Kings for granted.

4) We are one of the oldest teams in the league. Veterans were exhausted at playoff time.

2002 Strategy:

1) We need to prepare physically and mentally for the Stanley Cup tournament.
2) We need to engage our fans. They have come to take winning for granted.
3) We need to add younger legs and a reliable backup goalie for the playoffs.

Figure 8.11   Red Wings strategic plan. *(continued)*

2002 Action Plan														
2002 Goals	**2002 Activities**	**Schedule (Month)**												
		1	2	3	4	5	6	7	8	9	10	11	12	
A. Prepare physically and mentally *All players get physicals 2 weeks before playoffs*	1) Check conditioning 2) Make countermeaures for each player 3) Retain sports psychologist 4) Individual and team interventions													
B. Psych up our fans *One media event every 2 weeks for the duration of the playoffs*	1) Retain Pavarotti for all home games 2) Apply the "us against the world" routine 3) Mascot to go berserk at all play stoppings 4) Voodoo priestess to put hex on Avalanche													
C. Psych out our opponents *One voodoo hex per opponent* *Four ties to receive magic*	1) Goalie to go crazy before crucial games 2) Sand-bag the last month of season 3) Witch doctor puts magic in coach's ties 4) Voodoo priestess hexes on Avalanche													
D. Strengthen our team	1) Add Bobby Clobber from goon league 2) Add young legs with Cup experience 3) Add experienced backup goalie													

Follow-up/Unresolved issues
1) Confirm Pavarotti for crucial games.
2) How reliable is witch doctor and voodoo hex?
3) What if goalie really does go crazy before crucial game? Do psychological assessment.
4) Avalanche has retained Evil Eye expert. How to combat?

Figure 8.11 (continued)   Red Wings strategic plan.

Hoshin Implementation

This refers to the management activities required to implement the hoshins developed and involves applying the various PDCA cycles. There should be both formal and informal reviews throughout the year to make the current status and countermeasures visible.

Hoshin Evaluation

This refers to the year-end assessment of each hoshin. Were process and outcome goals achieved? If so, ask why five times. If not, also ask why five times. What did we learn? How can we strengthen our capabilities? This is what it means to be a learning organization.

Book of Knowledge

Annual hoshins for key goal areas (e.g., productivity, quality, safety, cost, and environment) should be kept in the department "Book of Knowledge." Thus, we will have a clear accessible history of our activities and challenges, another hallmark of a learning organization.

DOING THE RIGHT THINGS VERSUS DOING THINGS RIGHT

There is nothing more wasteful than doing efficiently what should not have been done at all.

Peter Drucker

Effectiveness versus efficiency: an eternal challenge. Those of us who have grown up in manufacturing naturally lean toward the latter. We know how to do things right, how to reduce the eight forms of waste, and thereby lead time. And indeed, efficiency (aka execution, and operational excellence) often trumps everything. But not always.

What if efficiency is not the constraint? Can you think of any value streams that are inefficient, but still fabulously successful? Let me give you a hint: iPod, iPhone, and iPad!

Are Apple's value streams the most efficient? Is the iPad, for example, as well built, as, say, a Toyota Corolla? (By "well built", I mean quality, lead time, and cost.) If you have teenage daughters, as I do, you may already know the answer. Try dropping your iPad a few times!

But Apple's design is so transcendent, it doesn't matter. When Steve Jobs unveiled the iPad, everybody wanted one. Price and robustness were not an issue. In this market, therefore, effectiveness trumps efficiency.

I don't want to be misunderstood. I am not saying that efficiency is of no consequence. (In fact, Samsung's combination of strong design plus robust manufacturing is challenging Apple.) Hoshin planning requires finesse. We have to take both effectiveness and efficiency into account.

Summary

Hoshin planning is the nervous system of Lean production. Through hoshin planning we seek to align our resources behind worthy goals. The hoshin planning system comprises PDCA, catchball, nemawashi, the control department concept, and A3 thinking. There are four phases to hoshin planning: development, deployment, implementation, and review. Strategies and tactics must be translated into meaningful action, level by level. Strengthening people is an important goal of hoshin planning. A common mistake is to take on too much. Pick a few boulders to work on each year.

Endnotes

1. Miyamoto Musashi was Japan's greatest swordsman. His guide for samurai warriors, *A Book of Five Rings* (Woodstock, NY: Overlook Press, 1982), has become a business strategy classic.
2. Thomas Homer-Dixon, *The Ingenuity Gap* (Toronto: Vintage Canada, 2001).
3. Michael Cowley and Ellen Domb, *Beyond Strategic Vision* (Boston: Butterworth-Heinemann, 1997).
4. Peter Senge, *The Fifth Discipline* (New York: Doubleday, 1990).
5. SMART stands for simple, measurable, achievable, reasonable, and trackable.
6. Special thanks to our late, lamented colleague Al Ward for the use of these symbols. We miss you Al.
7. Hoshin planning is also known as strategy deployment and policy deployment. For more information see Pascal Dennis, *Getting the Right Things Done: A Leader's Guide to Planning and Execution* (Cambridge, MA: Lean Enterprise Institute, 2006).
8. Ibid.
9. A hoshin is a strategy to achieve a higher-level goal.
10. Peter Drucker, *The Practice of Management* (New York: HarperCollins, 1954).

11. Yoji Akai, *Hoshin Kanri* (Portland, OR: Productivity Press, 1988).
12. Discussion with Toyota executive.
13. And if you fail, watch out!
14. Discussion with Toyota executive.
15. Discussion with Toyota executive.
16. Strategy means long-term plan. Tactic means short-term activity in support of a strategy.
17. Discussion with Toyota executive.
18. The term "control department" gives some people heartburn, so I often use "key thinker" or "pacemaker" (not to be confused with the pacemaker process in a value stream).
19. Pascal Dennis, *Getting the Right Things Done: A Leader's Guide to Strategy Deployment* (Cambridge, MA: Lean Enterprise Institute, 2006).
20. Toyota training document.
21. Yoji Akai, *Hoshin Kanri* (Portland, OR: Productivity Press, 1988).
22. Toyota training document.
23. Toyota training document.
24. Yoji Akai, *Hoshin Kanri* (Portland, OR: Productivity Press, 1988).
25. The assembly department is setting a more ambitious goal than the 20% suggested by senior management. This would be based on grasping its current capabilities and challenges.
26. I chose the Detroit Red Wings because many of our clients are Red Wings fans and I do not wish to further jinx my beloved Maple Leafs, now 48 years without a Stanley Cup victory.

Study Questions

1. What is planning?
2. Provide at least five examples of knowledge waste.
   a. What causes knowledge waste?
   b. What are possible countermeasures?
3. Describe your organization's strategic planning process.
   a. What are its strengths and weaknesses?
   b. How might you improve it?
4. Define "routine" and "improvement" work.
   a. Provide at least three examples of each in your organization.
   b. Provide at least one example each of point, flow, and system improvement.
5. Draw out the Strategy A3 storyboard and describe each section.
6. Why is it important to reflect on both outcomes and process?
7. What is the most important word in hoshin planning?
   a. Explain your answer.
   b. Why do organizations have a hard time using this word in strategy development?
   c. How might we make it easier to do so?

Chapter 9

The Culture
of Lean Production

They dance best who dance with desire.

Irving Layton

Intensity is the soul of Lean production, and team members are its heart. I had experienced intensity before I got to Toyota, the intensity of continual firefighting. Indeed, in many organizations people are valued according to their firefighting ability. Toyota's intensity is a different thing altogether.

I found that human resources (HR), a peripheral department in many organizations, is central at Toyota because it provides the most important input: people. HR has to address difficult questions:

- What qualities do we seek in our team members?
- How do we recruit such people?
- How do we train and develop them?
- How do we retain them?
- How do we motivate them?
- Through what activities do we involve them?
- How will we measure each of these parameters?

Moreover, at Toyota HR is the control department for core goals including

- Health and safety
- Training and development
- Culture

In some Toyota plants HR also functions as the control department for hoshin planning.

The implication is clear: HR is vital to Lean success and must learn to apply Lean thinking, and especially the PDCA cycle, to all its activities.

What Is Lean Culture?

The constraint is not technology, it's governance.

Thomas Homer-Dixon

What is organizational culture? In my experience it is

- The day-to-day experience of our team members
- Current behavior

I have visited Toyota plants on several continents. Day-to-day experience and behavior in each includes the following:

- Plan-do-check-act
- Standardization
- Visual management
- Teamwork
- Paradox
- Intensity
- The do[1] concept

PDCA

PDCA is the core activity of management.[2] Here are the corollaries:

- A manager's job is to practice and teach PDCA.
- The best managers practice PDCA on a daily basis.
- PDCA thinking must inform all our activities from day-to-day kaizen, to problem solving, to strategic planning.

PDCA is deceptively simple. But there are many levels of understanding that take a lifetime to fully grasp. PDCA is best learned by doing under the guidance of strong senseis. Thus, HR must also ask, "How will we support mentoring in our organization?"

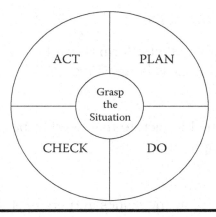

Figure 9.1   PDCA cycle.

Deming introduced PDCA to the Japanese in his 1954 lectures to the Japanese Union of Scientists and Engineers. Deming credited his mentor Walter Shewhart, upon whose initial research-design-produce-sell cycle PDCA was based. Figure 9.1 illustrates the PDCA cycle.

Let us briefly review each PDCA component to illustrate the levels of understanding.

PDCA AND WAKEFULNESS

"We live our lives asleep," is a recurrent theme in the great religions and philosophies. In my coaching work, I call it "The Fog." Those of you who work in large corporations may know what I mean. Everything is blurry, including our purpose, processes, and expected outcomes. Visual management and other forms of communication are sketchy, so we're unable to answer the most basic questions: "What game are we playing? Who are our customers? What do they need from us? What is today's work? Are we winning or losing?"

PDCA is about wakefulness. It's full of embedded tests meant to counter the anesthetizing fog. For example, plan phase tests include

- Have we defined the purpose of our plan or activity clearly?
- Have we linked our purpose to our organization's overall purpose?
- Do we have a clear picture of our current condition?
- Do we have a clear picture of our target condition?
- Is our plan doable with our current resources?

Thus, PDCA continually nudges us, "Hey, wake up!"

Grasping the Situation (GTS)

GTS is a continuous activity that informs each PDCA step. GTS entails developing a problem consciousness by grasping:

■ The big picture
■ The key parts of the big picture that need to be deeply investigated
■ What is actually happening
■ What should be happening
■ Current and likely future trends
■ How the issue relates to the values and goals of the organization

GTS is an active process that requires nemawashi and going to see the actual condition. GTS is much easier if we have developed SMART goals and good measurement systems.

Plan

To plan we must determine

■ Where do we want to go?
■ How do we get there?

Nemawashi and going to the shop floor to see are also required to answer these questions fully. A good plan must include the following elements:

■ 5 Ws and 1 H: who, what, when, where, why, and how
■ Measurement plan including SMART goals, hassle-free measurement processes, and visual systems for shared understanding

Related questions include

■ What good and bad things could happen along the way, and how will we react?
■ What is the current capability of our people?
■ What training is required to raise their capability?
■ What are the checkpoints and milestones along the way?

Important outputs of planning are the Gantt chart, contingency plan, and control panels or dashboards.

Do

Do contains its own PDCA cycle (Figure 9.2). This reflects the importance of pilot activities. A good pilot allows us to strengthen and confirm our plan before full implementation. This approach contrasts with the "just do it" mindset.

As noted, PDCA requires a sober assessment of the capability of team members. Capability gaps have to be filled before the do step. This in turn requires sound methods for measuring team member capability. HR must have a concrete image of what that capability "looks like" so that we can assess our current condition and make countermeasures.

Check

Check also means confirm. Therefore, we must decide

- Whom to check with
- What to check
- When to check
- How frequently to check
- In what manner to check

Sound measurement facilitates checking by making problems immediately obvious. Metrics must address both outcomes (final score) and the processes by which these are achieved. A good metaphor is football. We want to know the

- Outcome: final score
- Process: first downs, passing yards, rushing yards, interceptions, and fumbles

Process results help us to improve.

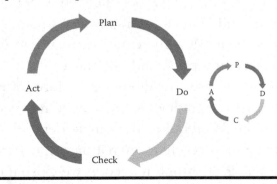

Figure 9.2   The do PDCA cycle.

"Go see" is also fundamental. We must not rely on paper reports or hearsay. We must go see what is actually happening. We must eliminate the possibility of failure through checking.

Act

Act means reflecting on our condition after checking and taking appropriate action, including

- Standardize when both outcome and process results are on target.
- Make countermeasures when either outcome or process results are substandard.

Experience shows that we usually need to take countermeasures. These should include both

- Temporary action to "stop the bleeding"
- Permanent countermeasures, which address the root cause

We must also maintain our people focus in the act phase, by reflecting on capability gaps and future training needs.

Reflection—Breakfast of Champions

Reflection, *hansei* in Japanese, is central to PDCA's act phase. It entails much more than asking, "How did we do?" Reflection entails honest humble acceptance of successes and failures, strengths and weaknesses, and a sincere commitment to do better. It is the countermeasure to *hubris*, the Greek word that means overweening pride and arrogance.

Reflection is central to all great religions, in the form of prayer, meditation, and rumination. In some traditions, the acolyte reflects in solitude. In my experience, reflection also requires the camaraderie of one's team so we can share our learning. Questions like, "'What have I learned?" naturally lead to, "What have *we* learned?" Through reflection we close the PDCA loop, and lay the foundation for the next PDCA cycle.

Warm Heart Principle

PDCA is a severe taskmaster. We must be also informed by the warm heart principle: "Hard on the problem, easy on the people."

Managers must recognize their responsibility to strengthen their team members. Good managers recognize the difference between stretching their team members, which helps them grow, and overloading, which does damage.

THE LIGHT TOUCH

The "light touch" is an important part of the warm heart principle. Change is hard; change hurts. Change is nobody's constituency, whereas the status quo is everyone's. Yet, in an ever-challenging world, change and continuous improvement are necessary. How do we help our team members acclimatize to it? We need to lead with a "light touch," informed by the following beliefs:

- Most people are decent and hardworking and want do what's right.
- Most of the problem is in the system, not the people.
- Change is hardest for middle management.
- Humor helps the medicine go down.
- People learn best when they're laughing.

The light touch expresses fundamental decency and respect for people, absent which, you can't sustain much. I've seen it turn many a sour grumbler into an "OK, I'll try" doer, and some into "Follow me!" champions.

Change is hard; change hurts. Remember the light touch.

Standardization

We discussed standardization in Chapters 3 and 4. Let me reiterate the key point. In the Lean system a standard is a robust shop floor tool that is meant to change continually as we discover better ways of doing our work. A standard, therefore, is merely our best current method, a temporary stopping point in our endless quest for perfection.

Therefore, you should feel free to write all over your standards. Record and date your changes. Don't reprint them every time. A standard's evolution is almost as important as its current form.

Problem Solving

A problem is a deviation from a standard, that is, a difference between what should be happening and what's actually happening.

What should be happening? (Standard)

Gap = Problem

What is actually happening?

At Toyota we learned a simple and elegant problem-solving process based on the following funnel image:

Problem-Solving Funnel

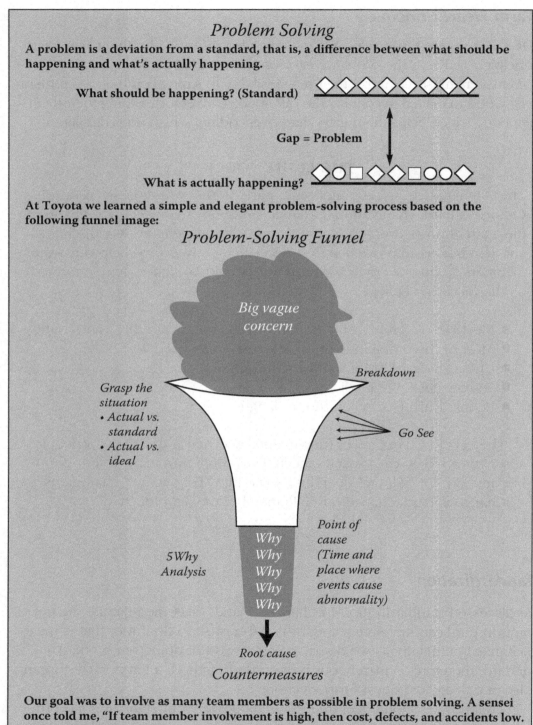

Big vague concern

Breakdown

Grasp the situation
- *Actual vs. standard*
- *Actual vs. ideal*

Go See

5 Why Analysis

Why
Why
Why
Why
Why

Point of cause (Time and place where events cause abnormality)

Root cause

Countermeasures

Our goal was to involve as many team members as possible in problem solving. A sensei once told me, "If team member involvement is high, then cost, defects, and accidents low. But if involvement is low…"

Standards and Abnormality Control

Our standards must make the out-of-standard condition obvious. Here is a simple example. If your workplace is a pigsty, then you will be unable to spot an abnormality, such as a banana peel on the floor or a leak beneath a piece of equipment.

If, by contrast, your standard is to have a spotless workplace, then the out-of-standard condition—the banana peel or the leak—is immediately obvious and can be quickly fixed.

FIVE WHY ANALYSIS

At Toyota, Five Why analysis is a core problem-solving tool. We were taught to ask why continually until we found the root cause of a problem. This entails moving up and down a "ladder of abstraction" from an abstract gap (in throughput) to concrete observations.

Five Why requires practice; it's easy to end up far away from the actual root cause. Here is a useful rule of thumb: root causes invariably fall into one of three categories:

- Inadequate standard
- Inadequate adherence to standard
- Inadequate system

Here is an example, which legend has it, came out of Taiichi Ohno's Kamigo Engine plant:

Problem Statement

What made 900 units versus a target of 1,200? Why?
Because the robot stopped. Why?
Because it was overloaded and a fuse blew. Why?
Because the arm wasn't properly lubricated. Why?
Because the lubrication pump wasn't working right. Why?
Because dirt and debris got into the pump shaft. Why?
Because the pump motor was designed without a filter.

The root cause of the breakdown would likely be either "inadequate standard"; that is, we didn't realize the pump motors should have filters to prevent debris from getting into the pump shaft, or "inadequate adherence to standard"; that is, we had a standard, we just didn't follow it.

Visual Management

Visual management means more pictures and fewer words, so as to satisfy the visual management triangle (Figure 3.1).

Management as Theater

Visual management also means public presentations to ensure shared understanding. At Toyota I came to understand management as theater. Each week we partook in shop floor events designed to make problems visible. These included

- Line-side process reviews
- Safety or quality "auctions"[3]
- Current condition presentations at team member information centers
- Hoshin planning presentations

I remember thinking, "I can run, but I cannot hide." If I was messing up, everyone knew it. Conversely, because all managers were equally "naked," we generally supported each other.

Teamwork

"All for one and one for all" is a stirring mantra. At Toyota we went to great lengths to promote it:

- *Safety first.* Safety is a core value on a par with production and quality. Safety is also good business. Poor ergonomics, for example, inevitably leads to quality and productivity problems.[4]
- *Employment security.* There is an implicit guarantee to the effect that only in the most severe circumstances and as a last resort would job cutbacks be considered.
- *Uniforms.* All team members wear the same uniform irrespective of position.
- *No executive offices and no walls.* Toyota offices are typically one large room containing rows of desks. Managers, technical specialists, and executives typically sit elbow to elbow.[5]
- *No executive dining rooms or parking spaces.*
- *Genchi genbutsu.* The "go see" spirit ensures that managers and senior managers are in constant contact with shop floor team members.

Of course, these will not fit in every organization. We must tailor our activities to our culture.

Employment security may not be a realistic goal, especially in a brown-field facility. If job cuts are required, my advice is as follows:

■ Be honest. Explain the choices. Either we lose some jobs or we lose them all.
■ Offer fair severance packages.
■ Use targeted buyouts (and keep the best people!).
■ Once the optimal headcount has been reached, commit to employment security.

KAIZEN SPIRIT

A humane indomitable spirit animates the Lean system. This "kaizen spirit" comprises three things:

1. *Cheerfulness:* We believe that, no matter how tough things are today, tomorrow will be better. We'll keep improving, and we'll solve our most difficult problems.
2. *Go see:* We experience things firsthand. We get out of the office and into the Gemba. We work with frontline team members with respect and humility.
3. *Get your hands dirty:* We learn by doing. We roll up our sleeves and try stuff. We run experiments to prove cause and effect. Then we lock in countermeasures with standardized work and visual management. Lastly, we share what we've learned.

Let me expand on cheerfulness. I'm not referring to the Pollyanna variety: shallow, rootless, ill-informed by life. I mean deeply rooted cheerfulness, informed of life's ups and downs, and wearing a sunny smile nonetheless. Cheerfulness is a statement: "Yes, life is tough and there are plenty of reasons to be depressed. But here we are, making things a little better every day, in spite of everything!"

I remember my old aikido sensei cupping his hands on his chest. "You must have a big heart, Pascal-san!" It's all the same.

Paradox

I found the Toyota system to be full of paradoxes, and therefore endlessly engaging. Here are but a few examples:

- Jidoka. Stop production so that production never has to stop.
- Standards change all the time.
- One-at-a-time production is more effective than batch production.
- Maximizing unit efficiencies does not maximize overall efficiency.
- Don't make something unless a customer has ordered it.
- Team members, not industrial engineers, develop standardized work.
- Seek perfection, even though we know we will never achieve it.

Therefore, I learned to approach the system with humility, recognizing that it may take a lifetime to grasp. It took a while to shed the "been there, done that" mentality that closes the door to profound knowledge and growth.

Intensity

PDCA, standardization, visual management, the endless quest for perfection, and so on, make for an intense culture. There is no place to hide, no downtime. Intensity compels kaizen. In the absence of kaizen, a Lean manager's workload may be 90 hours per week. You quickly learn what has value and what is muda (Figure 9.3). You learn how to develop robust systems and how to manage abnormalities. You learn the Lean tools and concepts because you need to.

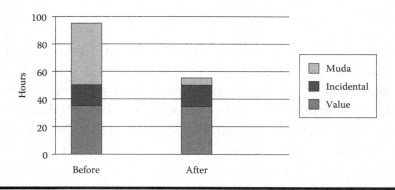

Figure 9.3   Intensity compels kaizen.

The same is true of shop floor processes. Initially, processes are full of muda and team members may struggle to keep up. Rather than throw resources at the problem, we must identify the muda and make kaizen. We might provide support in the short term. Again, intensity compels kaizen.

There are important ramifications for Lean implementation. With our clients I have learned to ask:

■ How will we prepare our people to handle intensity?
■ What are the needed skills?
■ How will we handle requests for more resources?

Managers must stay close to their teams and recognize the symptoms of strain. Provide support as required, but maintain the intensity. Over time, as we eliminate muda, work becomes easier.

Lean Production as a Path

When a set of methods or techniques connects to a person's whole being, it becomes a do or path. Examples include kendo, judo, and aikido. I have come to understand that the Toyota system is a do. Therefore, we must approach it with the proper spirit:

■ *Humility.* We seek but know we will never achieve perfection.
■ *Life-long learning.*
■ *Respect for people.* Leaders must ask, "How can I strengthen my team members?"

Walking a path provides tremendous energy, clarity, and purpose to one's life. I am struck by the longevity of the great senseis: Deming, Ohno, Juran, Ishikawa, Shingo, Feigenbaum, and others.

How Does Lean Culture Feel?

As I reflect on my Toyota experience, here are some words that come to mind:

■ Disciplined
■ Freewheeling

- Warm
- Indomitable

PDCA provides both scientific discipline and the freewheeling spirit of inquiry that asks: "How can we do this better?" Respect for people creates pleasing warmth and camaraderie. Team members interact as equals. "Them versus us" does not exist. Meeting daunting challenges year after year gives us confidence in the future.

This then is the culture of Lean production, the soil in which this remarkable system thrives. In your Lean implementation efforts, please reflect on these ideas and take action to improve.

Summary

The culture of Lean production comprises PDCA, standardization, visual management, teamwork, intensity, paradox, and Lean production as a do or path. PDCA is the core tool of management and requires years to fully grasp. Standardization supports abnormality control. We seek to satisfy the visual management triangle so as to create a shared understanding among all team members. Visual management also means management as theater. Lean production is not merely a set of techniques. By connecting to our whole being it becomes a path, which creates energy, focus, and longevity.

Final Comments

> To suggest is to create. To define is to destroy.
>
> **Garcia Lorca**

I began my Lean journey 25 years ago. Like many others I began with a gut feeling that there had to be a better way to manage. We spend so much of our lives at work. Why shouldn't it fulfill our deepest needs?

The journey has transformed me. As I reflect at midcareer, I recognize that the Lean system cannot and should not be precisely defined. There is no one right path, no one correct answer. There is only the question: What is the need?

The best we can do is to practice and teach our team members the central concepts, knowing that they'll develop them further. Each of us must make the journey from "Thou shalt" to "What do you think?"

I leave you, therefore with the image with which I began this book: that is, of a journey toward Lean production.

Bon voyage.

Endnotes

1. *Do* means way or path. A set of activities becomes a path when it connects to a person's whole being.
2. Discussion with Toyota executive.
3. An "auction" is a standardized presentation of an investigation into a safety or quality incident. Attendees may ask questions, give advice, or offer to help the investigators.
4. For a detailed discussion of the link between safety, quality, and productivity please refer to *Quality, Safety & Environment: Synergy in the 21st Century* (Milwaukee: ASQ Quality Press, 1997), available through 1-800-248-1946.
5. This takes some getting used to.

Study Questions

1. What is Human Resources responsible for in a Lean organization?
2. How well does your organization practice PDCA?
   a. What might your organization do to improve?
3. The author suggests that "PDCA and Lean are about wakefulness."
   a. What is his rationale?
   b. Do you agree or disagree with it? Explain your thinking.
4. What is *hansei* and why is it important in a Lean organization?
5. Define kaizen spirit.
   a. How does an organization sustain it?
   b. What are the obstacles to sustaining kaizen spirit?
   c. What are possible countermeasures?
6. Describe your organization's problem-solving process.
   a. What makes it effective (or ineffective)?
   b. How might your organization improve?
7. In what ways is Lean a "path" or do?
   a. What are some of the challenges of walking a "path"?
   b. How does a person sustain his or her commitment to a "path"?

Glossary

Lean production constitutes a language, much of which is Japanese. In my work, I have found a fairly even split between people who like the Japanese terms and others who prefer their English equivalents. I have developed the following glossary to accommodate both groups.

Japanese words tend to be visual and metaphorical. Often there are no English equivalents. I have tried to provide the nearest equivalent English term, as well as the most vivid metaphor to convey the meaning as closely as possible.

4 Ms: Man/woman, machine, material, and method.

Affinity diagram: A tool for gathering and grouping ideas; one of the new seven quality tools; used in hoshin planning.

Andon: A line stop; typically a cord that a worker can pull to stop the assembly line when he or she detects a defect; an example of jidoka.

Cell: An arrangement of people, machines, materials, and methods such that processing steps are adjacent and in sequential order so that parts can be processed one at a time (or in some cases in a consistent small batch that is maintained through the process sequence). The purpose of a cell is to achieve and maintain efficient continuous flow.

Continuous flow: In its purest form continuous flow means that items are processed and moved directly to the next process one piece at a time. Each processing step completes its work just before the next process needs the item, and the transfer batch size is one. Also known as one-piece flow and "make one, move one."

Deshi: Student.

Dojo: Training hall.

Fishbone diagram: A problem-solving and brainstorming tool; also known as a cause and effect diagram; one of the seven quality tools.

Five S: A system of workplace standardization and organization. The five Ss are sort, set in order, shine, standardize, and sustain.

Five Why analysis: A problem-solving technique that entails continually asking why until the root cause is found.

Gemba: The real place or the specific place. Usually means the shop floor and other areas where work is done.

Genchi genbutsu: Go see; go to the real place and see what is actually happening.

GTS: Grasp the situation; the heart of PDCA.

Hansei: Reflection; part of both hoshin planning and problem solving; entails honest humble acceptance of successes and failures, strengths and weaknesses, and a sincere commitment to do better.

Heijunka: Production leveling.

Hoshin: A statement of objectives, goals, direction, and/or policy.

Hoshin kanri: A strategic planning system developed in Japan and North America over the past 30 years. Also known as Strategy Deployment. Metaphorical meanings include "ship in a storm going in the right direction" and "shining needle or compass."

Hoshin planning: See Hoshin kanri.

Jidoka: Automation with a human mind. Jidoka means developing processes with both high capability (few defects made) and containment (defects contained in the zone).

Jishuken: Voluntary study groups; for example, association suppliers might join to share experiences and thus deepen their understanding of critical concepts.

Kaizen: A small incremental improvement. Kaizen activity should involve everyone regardless of position.

Kanban: A small sign or signboard, an instruction to produce or supply something; usually a card; usually includes supplier and customer names, and information on transportation and storage; a central element of the just-in-time system. There are two types: production and withdrawal kanbans.

Management by objectives (MBO): The precursor to hoshin planning; introduced by Peter Drucker in his 1954 book, *The Practice of Management* (HarperCollins).

Mental model: One's assumptions about how the world works, based on experience, temperament, and upbringing; the invisible glasses that filter our experience and determine what we see.

Muda: Waste.

Mura: Unevenness.

Muri: Strain, either physical or mental; overburden.

Nemawashi: Literally means "to prepare a tree for transplanting;" refers to the formal and informal method of gaining consensus prior to the implementation of a hoshin or plan.

New seven: Problem-solving tools developed in Japan and North America in the 1970s. They include the affinity diagram, fault tree, process decision program charts (PDPC), matrix, tree diagram, interrelationship digraph, and Gantt chart.

Pareto chart: A problem-solving tool comprising a bar chart showing possible contributing factors in descending order; one of the seven quality tools.

PDCA: The plan, do, check, act cycle developed by Walter Shewhart in the 1930s and refined by W. Edwards Deming.

Poka-yoke: An inexpensive robust device that eliminates the possibility of a defect by alerting the operator that an error has occurred.

Pull: To produce an item only when the customer asks for it. Typically, the customer "withdraws" the item and we "plug the gap" created thereby.

Push: To produce an item irrespective of actual demand; creates the muda of overproduction.

SMART: Simple, measurable, achievable, reasonable, and trackable. Refers to goals and targets.

Sensei: Teacher, one who has gone before.

Seven quality tools: Problem-solving tools developed in Japan and North America over the past century. They include the run chart, Pareto chart, histogram, control chart, checksheet, and scatter diagram.

Standard: The best way we know at this moment; standards in the Lean system change as we discover better ways of working; a clear simple image of what should be happening.

Store: A controlled inventory of items that is used to schedule production at an upstream process. Usually located near the upstream process to make customer requirements visible. Also called a supermarket.

Strategy deployment: See Hoshin kanri.

Supermarket: See Store.

Takt: The pace of production synchronized with the rate of sales.

Tree diagram: A tool used for mapping tasks for implementation; one of the new seven quality tools; used in hoshin planning.

Total productive maintenance (TPM): An integrated set of activities aimed at maximizing equipment effectiveness by involving everyone in all departments at all levels, typically through small-group activities. TPM usually entails implementing the 5S system, measuring the six big losses, prioritizing problems, and applying problem solving with the goal of achieving zero breakdowns.

Value stream: The series of steps required to bring a product or service to the customer.

Value stream map: A diagram, usually hand-drawn that shows the series of steps required to bring a product or service to a customer; also known as material and information flow diagram.

Work-in-process (WIP): Items between machines waiting to be processed.

Yokoten: Information sharing across the plant; sharing of common issues and countermeasures.

Bibliography

I have found the books below particularly helpful in understanding the Lean system.

5S System and Visual Management

Galsworth, Gwen. *Visual Systems: Harnessing the Power of a Visual Workplace.* New York: AMACOM, 1997.

Greif, Michel. *The Visual Factory: Building Participation Through Shared Information.* New York: Productivity Press, 1991.

Hirano, Hiroyuki. *5 Pillars of the Visual Workplace.* New York: Productivity Press, 1990.

Hirano, Hiroyuki. *Putting 5S to Work: A Practical Step by Step Guide.* Tokyo: PHP Institute, 1993.

Total Productive Maintenance

Hartmann, Edward. *Successfully Installing TPM in a Non-Japanese Plant.* Allison Park, PA: TPM Press, 1992.

Japan Institute of Plant Maintenance. *TPM for Every Operator.* New York: Productivity Press, 1996.

Nakajima, Seiichi. *Introduction to TPM.* New York: Productivity Press, 1988.

Jidoka

NKS/Factory Magazine. *Poka-yoke: Improving Quality by Preventing Defects.* New York: Productivity, Press 1988.

Shingo, Shigeo. *Zero Quality Control: Source Inspection and the Poka-yoke System.* New York: Productivity Press, 1986.

Just-In-Time and Toyota Production System

Japanese Management Association. *Kanban: Just-In-Time at Toyota.* New York: Productivity Press, 1989.

Monden, Yasuhiro. *Toyota Production System: An Integrated Approach to Just-in-Time, 2nd edition.* Norcross, GA: EMP, 1993.

Ohno, Taiichi. *Toyota Production System: Beyond Large-Scale Production.* New York: Productivity Press, 1988.

Shingo, Shigeo. *A Study of the Toyota Production System from an Industrial Engineering Viewpoint.* New York: Productivity Press, 1989.

Toyota Motor Corporation. *The Toyota Production System.* Operations Management Consulting Division and International Public Affairs Division. Toyota City, Japan: Toyota Motor Corporation, 1995.

Value Stream Mapping

Rother, Mike, and John Shook. *Learning to See: Value Stream Mapping to Add Value and Eliminate Muda.* Brookline, MA: The Lean Enterprise Institute, 1999.

Continuous Flow

Harris, Rick, and Mike Rother. *Creating Continuous Flow: An Action Guide for Managers, Engineers and Production Associates.* Brookline, MA: The Lean Enterprise Institute, 2001.

Sekine, Kenichi. *One-Piece Flow: Cell Design for Transforming the Production Process.* New York: Productivity Press, 1994.

Hoshin Planning

Akao,Yoji. *Hoshin Kanri.* New York: Productivity Press, 1990.

Cowley, Michael, and Ellen Domb. *Beyond Strategic Vision: Effective Corporate Action with Hoshin Planning.* Newton, MA: Butterworth-Heinemann, 1997.

Dennis, Pascal. *Getting the Right Things Done: A Leader's Guide to Planning and Execution.* Cambridge, MA: LEI Press, 2006.

Systems Thinking

Dennis, Pascal. *The Remedy: Bringing Lean Out of the Factory to Transform the Entire Organization.* New York: Wiley, 2010.

Goldratt, Eliyahu. *The Goal: A Process of Ongoing Improvement, 2nd edition.* Great Barrington, MA: North River Press, 1992.

Homer-Dixon, Thomas. *The Ingenuity Gap: Can We Solve the Problems of the Future.* Toronto: Vintage Canada, 2001.

Scholtes, Peter. *The Leader's Handbook: A Guide to Inspiring Your People and Managing the Daily Workflow.* New York: McGraw-Hill, 1998.

Senge, Peter. *The Fifth Discipline: The Art & Practice of the Learning Organization.* New York: Doubleday, 1990.

Senge, Peter, et al. *The Dance of Change: The Challenge of Sustaining Momentum in Learning Organizations.* New York: Doubleday, 1990.

Lean Thinking

Dennis, Pascal. *Andy & Me: Crisis and Transformation on the Lean Journey, 2nd edition,* New York: Taylor & Francis, 2011.

Dennis, Pascal. *The Remedy: Bringing Lean Out of the Factory to Transform the Entire Organization.* New York: Wiley, 2010.

Liker, Jeffrey, (Editor). *Becoming Lean: Inside Stories of US Manufacturers.* New York: Productivity Press, 1998.

Womack, James, and Daniel Jones. *Lean Thinking: Banish Waste and Create Wealth in Your Corporation.* New York: Simon & Schuster, 1996.

Womack, James, Daniel Jones, and Daniel Roos. *The Machine That Changed the World.* New York: Simon & Schuster, 1990.

Leadership and Ethics

Dennis, Pascal. *Reflections of a Business Nomad: Stories and Poems from the Road.* Toronto: Skopelos Press, 2012.

Index

4 Ms, 39, 66
  stabilizing, 40
5 Ws and 1 H, 194
5S system, 24–25, 39, 42, 44
  set in order, 47–48
  shine and inspect, 49
  sort, 45–47
  standardize, 49–51
  sustain, 51–52

A

A3 reports
  telling stories with, 179
  types of, 176–177
Abnormality control, 107, 199
Accounting practices, 6
Act, 196
Actual work, 29
Adjustment delays, 55
Affinity diagrams, 183
Alignment, 166, 168, 171–172
Andon process, 125
Annual culture hoshin, 158–159
Annual hoshins, 187
Annual jidoka strategy, 138
Assembly, coordination of, 3
Assembly line, 3
  moving, 4
Audit, 69
Automobiles
  craft production of, 2
  Ford system of manufacture, 3–4

Auxiliary work, 29
Availability, 54

B

Balance charts, 79–80
Batch production, 7, 93
Binary connections, 102
Book of knowledge, 187
Bottlenecks, eliminating, 82
Breakdown, 58
Breakdown maintenance, 54
Business processes, value stream mapping
      and, 118–119

C

Capability gaps, 195
Capable processes, 96
Capacity planning, 91
Capital asset disposal, 46
Catchball, 172–173
Cause and effect diagrams, 181
Cells, 71–72, 84
  benefit of, 86
  determining the number of operators in,
      81
Changeover, 79
Check, 195–196
Cleaning, 49
Color standard, 48
Communication, 52, 153
Connected islands, 84

Connected islands with full-work control, 84
Consensus building, 171–172
Contact sensors, 134
Contingency plans, 194
Continuous flow, 25, 34, 92–93
Control department concept, 174–176, 191–192
Control panels, 170, 194
Conventional mental models, 24
Conveyance
    kinds of, 107–108
    overproduction and, 33
    role of in JIT system, 105–108
    waste in, 32
Correction, 30
    overproduction and, 33
Cost reduction, 20
Counters, 133
Craft production, 1
    characteristics of, 1–2
Critical condition measures, 134
Culture hoshin, 158–159
Current status A3, 177–178
Customer demand
    responding to changes in, 110
    understanding, 108–109
Customer focus, 25, 28–29
Cycle times, 3, 90
    takt time and, 71–72

D

Dashboards, 194
Defects, 55
    common errors leading to, 127–128
    discovering, 128
    human error and, 124–127
    preventing, 129
    reducing, 129
Delays, 30
Demand
    changes in, 106
    understanding, 108–109
Deming, W. Edwards, 124, 193
Deployment phase of hoshin, 182
    output, 182–186

Deviations from fixed values, 133–134
Differential transformers, 134
Direct binary connections, 102
Disposal, 46
Do, 195
Downtime, 55
Drucker, Peter, 53, 168

E

Economics, effect of changes in, 19–21
Economy of motion, guidelines for, 82
Effectiveness vs. efficiency, 187–188
Efficiency
    effectiveness vs., 187–188
    improving, 78–79
    measure of, 68
    overall vs. individual, 80–82
Electric current fluctuations, 135
Element time, 79
Employee involvement, 10, 25, 34, 69
    activities supporting, 146
    goal of, 146–147
    kaizen circle activity (KCA), 148–152
    motivating people, 151–152
    practical kaizen training, 152–154
    rationale for, 143–144
    suggestion programs, 154–159
Employment security, 10
Engineering, mass production and, 7
Enterprise resource planning (ERP), 91
    lack of visual management in, 42
Equipment
    breakdowns, 55
    guidelines for, 82–83
Ergonomics, 72
    risk factors for injury, 30–31
Evaluation phase of hoshin, 187
Extrinsic motivation, 157

F

FIFO flow, 112–113
Fishbone diagrams, 181
Five why analysis, 199
Fixed values, deviations from, 133–134
Flexibility, 92, 166, 168

Flow, 40
  creating, 164
  muda and, 94
Flow improvement, 167
Fluctuations in work, 35, 79. *See also* Mura
Ford system, 3–4
Ford, Edsel, 4–5
Ford, Henry, 3–5
Full-work control, 132
  connected islands with, 84

G

Gantt charts, 194
Genchi genbutsu, 200–201
General Motors, 5–6
  partnership of with Toyota Motor
    Company, 11–12 (*See also* NUMMI)
Generally accepted accounting practice
    (GAAP), 6
Generation phase of hoshin, 180
Gilbreth, Frank, 65
Gilbreth, Lillian, 65
Go-see spirit, 200–201
Good–no good inspections, 128
Grasping the situation (GTS), 194

H

Hansei, 196
Hard to do, 36
Healthcare
  applicability of continuous flow to, 92–93
  use of jidoka in, 138–139
  use of kanban in, 104–105
  use of visual management in, 43
Heijunka, 35, 96. *See also* Production leveling
Heijunka box, 111
Heinrich, Herbert, 57
Hidden failure, 58
Hidden losses, 55–56
Hirano, Hiroyuki, 24
Home positions, 43
Homer-Dixon, Thomas, 161
Hoshin planning, 137, 165. *See also* Planning
  A3 report, 177–178
  alignment and flexibility, 166

catchball, 172–173
check outcomes and process, 170
control department concept, 174–176
focus of, 165–166
MBO and, 168
nemawashi, 171–172
outcome of, 173
PDCA, 169–170
phases of, 180–187
routine vs. improvement work, 166
strengthening people, 170–171
House of Lean Production, 25–26
Human error, 124–127
  rates of, 126
  use of jidoka to alleviate, 139
Human motion, 29
Human resources, necessity of for Lean
    culture, 191–192

I

Idling, 55
Imai, Masaaki, 58
Implementation phase of hoshin, 187
Improvement processes, 40
Improvement work, hoshin planning and, 166
In-process stock, 72–73
Individual efficiency, 80–82
Industrial engineering, 65–66
Informative inspections, 129
Ingenuity gap, 161
Inspect, 49
  standards for, 51
Inspection systems, 128
  informative inspections, 129
  judgment inspections, 128
Instability, sources of, 69, 106
Intangible suggestions, 156
Intensity, 191, 202
Interchangeability of parts, 3
Intrinsic motivation, 157
Inventory, 32–33
  overproduction and, 33
Involvement, 25, 34, 69
  activities supporting, 146
  employment security and, 10
  goal of, 146–147

motivating people, 151–152
practical kaizen training, 152–154
rationale for, 143–144
suggestion programs, 154–159
Islands, 84

J

Japan
Lean production in, 13
standards in, 40–41
Jidoka, 25
annual strategy and goal setting, 138
aspects of, 136–137
concept development, 123–124
implementing, 137–138
rationale for, 124–127
use of outside the factory, 138–139
Jigs, guidelines for, 83
JIT, 25, 39, 89
components of, 96
continuous flow, 92–93
dependence of on jidoka, 125
expanded role of conveyance, 105–108
kanban, 96–105
principles of, 92
production leveling and, 108–110
pull, 93–95
rationale for, 89–91
use of in office environments, 111–112
value stream mapping, 114–118
Job element sheets, 76
Job security, 145, 151–152
employee involvement and, 10
Jones, Daniel, 19, 25
Judgment inspections, 128
Just-in-time delivery. *See* JIT

K

Kaizen, 69, 79–80
Quick & Easy, 147
standardized work and, 82–83
value stream mapping and, 115–117
Kaizen circle activity (KCA), 148
administration, 149
promotion of, 150

role of the manager in, 151
roles and responsibilities, 149
sample report format, 150
targets for, 158–159
training, 148
Kaizen spirit, 201
Kanban, 92, 96–99
applicability of outside manufacturing,
104–105
direct binary connections and, 102
metaphors for, 99–100
pacemaker process, 100
rules of, 102–104
store, 101
Key thinkers, 174–175
Knowledge waste, 33–34, 161
types of, 164
Knowledge work, 53
Knowledge workers, standardized work for,
77–78

L

Labor density, 68
Labor movement, mass production and, 5–6
Labor relations, Japanese automotive
industry, 10
Language, use of in report writing, 179–180
Law of utilization, 114
Law of variability, 90
Law of variability buffering, 91
Lean
improvement processes, 40
use of in office environments, 52–53
Lean activities, 26
Lean culture, 192, 203–204
intensity, 202
paradoxes in, 202
PDCA, 192–196 (*See also* PDCA)
reflection, 196
standardization, 197 (*See also*
Standardization)
standards and abnormality control, 199
teamwork, 200–201
visual management, 200 (*See also* Visual
management)
warm heart principle, 197

Lean production
   basis of, 24–28
   birth of, 8–13
   customer focus, 28–29
   economics of, 19–21
   history of, 12–13
   house of, 25–26
   mental models, 24
   systems and systems thinking, 21–23
   use of in Japanese industry, 13
   use of outside of manufacturing, 14
Lean system standards, 39–42
   5S, 44–52 (*See also* 5S system)
   visual management, 42–44 (*See also*
     Visual management)
Lean thinking, methods engineering vs.,
   65–66
Light touch, 197
Limit switches, 134
Line-side process reviews, 170
Little's law, 90
Locations, 81
   rationalization of, 47–48

M

Machine Loss Pyramid, 57–58
Machine utilization, maximizing, 67
Machinery
   mass production and, 7
   measures of effectiveness of, 54
Maintenance, 54. *See also* TPM
   lifespan characteristics, 56
Management by objectives (MBO), 168
   emphasis of, 170
Managers, role of in KCA, 151
Manpower reduction, 78–80
Mass production, 2–3
   dysfunction of, 6–8
   labor movement and, 5–6
Material requirement planning. *See* MRP
Mean time between failure (MTBF), 55
Mean time to repair (MTTR), 55
Measuring success, 195
Mental models, 23–24
Metal passage detectors, 135
Method, definition of, 67

Methods engineering, Lean thinking vs.,
   65–66
Microswitches, 134
Minor failure, 58
Minor stoppages, 55, 58
Missing part methods, 133–134
Mixing models, 35
Monden, Yasuhiro, 25
Motion
   guidelines for economy of, 82
   overproduction and, 33
   waste of, 30–31
Motivating suggestions, 157–158
Move the metal mentality, 7
Moving assembly line, 4
MRP, 32–33, 91
   lack of visual management in, 42
Muda, 20, 29–30, 36
   categories of, 30–31
   conveyance, 32
   correction, 32
   delays, 30
   flow and, 94
   inventory, 32–33
   knowledge waste, 33–34
   overprocessing, 32
   overproduction, 33
   wasted motion, 30–31
   work vs., 29–30
Mura, 35–36
Muri, 36
Mutual respect, 145

N

Nakajima, Seiichi, 24
Nemawashi, 171–172, 194
New United Motor Manufacturing Inc. *See*
   NUMMI
Noncontact sensor methods, 134–135
NUMMI, 11–12
   5S at, 46–47

O

Office environments
   kanban in, 105

use of JIT in, 111–112
use of Lean in, 52–53
Ohba, Hajime, 14
Ohno, Taiichi, 8, 12, 25, 145
Operations Management Consulting
        Division (OMCD), 13–14
Operator balance chart, 79
Organizational learning, 69
Overall efficiency, 80–82
Overall equipment effectiveness (OEE), 54
    tracking, 55–56
Overprocessing, 32
Overproduction, 33

P

Pacemaker process, 100
PDCA, 169–171, 192–193
    act, 196
    check, 195–196
    do, 195
    grasping the situation, 194
    plan, 194
    wakefulness and, 193
People. *See also* Human error
    improving reliability of, 127
    maximizing utilization of, 67
    motivating, 151–152, 157–158
    standardized work and respect for, 83
    strengthening, 170–171
Performance efficiency, 54
Periodic work, 79
Photoelectric devices, 135
Pitch, 106
Plan, 194
Plan-do-check-act. *See* PDCA
Planning. *See also* Hoshin planning
    control department concept, 174–176
    definition of, 162
    problems with, 163–164
    rationale for, 163
Planning and execution tree, 173
Plant layout, 47–48, 81
    assessment of forms of, 85
    common forms of, 83–85
    guidelines for, 82–83
Point improvement, 167

Poka-yoke, 44, 69, 124, 127, 136–137
    actions, 131–132
    common errors, 127–128
    detection methods, 134–136
    effective, 131
    paths to, 132–134
PQCDSM, 66
Practical kaizen training, 152–153
    key factors for success, 153–154
Pressure sensors, 135
Preventive maintenance, 54
Price setting, 19–20
Problem solving, 69, 154, 198
    A3 report, 177
Process, definition of, 67
Process defects, 55
Process stability, 68
Production, stopping, 127, 130–131
Production capacity chart, 73–74
Production kanban, 97–98
Production leveling, 35, 96, 108–110
    example, 110
    heijunka box, 111
Production orders, frequency of, 106
Production physics, 90
Production plans, 100
Profit equation, 20
Promotion, 52
    kaizen circle activity, 150
    suggestion programs, 156–157
Proposal A3, 177
Pull systems, 30, 40, 93–95, 112
    control of WIP with, 95
    example, 99, 113
    Type A, 112
    Type B, 112–113
    Type C, 113
Push systems, 32–33, 89, 91

Q

Quality, mass production and, 7
Quasi-problems, 58
Queue production, 93
Quick & Easy kaizen, 147
Quick die changeover, 13, 96

R

Rationalize locations, 47–48
Rebalancing production, 79–80
Recycling, 46
Red tagging, 45–46
Reduced speed, 55
Reduced yield, 55
Reducing cost, 20
Reflection, 196
Repeaters, 109
Report boards, 170
Report writing
   common problems, 177
   history of, 176
   importance of language, 179–180
Rouge plant, 4, 8
Routine work, hoshin planning and, 166
Runners, 109

S

Safety, 151–152
Sekine, Kenichi, 25
Self-checking inspections, 129
Sensors
   contact, 134
   noncontact methods, 134–135
Set in order, 47
   organize and apply colors, 48
   rationalize locations, 47–48
   standards for, 51
Setup delays, 55
Shine, 49
   standards for, 51
Shingo, Shigeo, 25
Shutdown, 131–132
Single best way concept, 65–66
Single-minute exchange of dies (SMED), 25
Sloan, Alfred, 5–6
SMART goals, 170, 194
Social ingenuity, 161
Solar system model, 22
Sort, 45
   red tagging, 45–46
   standards for, 51

Source inspection, 124, 129
   horizontal, 129, 131
   vertical, 129
Speed losses, 55–56
Stability, 34, 68
   Lean system standards for, 39–42
   use of 5S for, 44–52
   use of TPM for, 53–55
   use of visual management for, 42–44
Stamping machines, 7
Standard work, overall vs. individual
   efficiency, 80–82
Standardization, 49–51, 197
Standardized work, 3, 39, 67
   analysis chart, 75–76
   benefits of, 68–69
   combination table, 74–75
   common layouts, 83–85
   components of, 70
   elements of, 71–73, 106
   job element sheets, 76
   kaizen and, 82–83
   knowledge workers and, 77–78
   manpower reduction, 78–80
   prerequisites for, 69–70
   production capacity chart, 73–74
   respect for people and, 83
   time measurement, 76–77
Standards, 39–42, 199
   ethical behavior, 152
   use of colors, 48
   work piece deviations, 132–133
Statistical process control (SPC), 124
Stopping the line, 127, 130–131
Store, 101
Strangers, 109
Strategic planning
   control department concept, 174–176
   problems with, 163–164
   rationale for, 163
   sample output, 185–186
Strategy development process, 181
Successive checking, 129
Supervisor, role of in practical kaizen
   training, 154
Supply chain, effect of Lean on, 13–14

Sustain, 51
  promotion and communication, 52
  training, 52
System improvement, 167
System model, 22
  actual practice and, 23
Systems, 21–22
  characteristics of, 21
Systems thinking, 22–23
Systems view, 66–67

T

Take Action on Accident Prevention, 58
Takt time, 68–69, 71, 106
  cycle time and, 71–72
Tangible suggestions, 155
Taylor, Fred Winslow, 2–3, 12, 65, 146
Teamwork, 200–201
Temperature sensors, 135
Thinking way, 23, 25
Throughput, 90
Time measurement, 76–77
Tools, guidelines for, 83
Top-down control, illusion of, 146
Total productive maintenance, TPM
Touch switches, 134
Toyoda, Eiji, 8–9
Toyoda, Kiichiro, 9
Toyoda, Sakichi, 124
Toyota Motor Company
  control department at, 191–192
  early challenges, 8–9
  key thinkers at, 175
  manpower reduction at, 80
  Operational Management Consulting
      Division, 13–14
  partnership of with General Motors,
      11–12 (*See also* NUMMI)
  production plans at, 100
Toyota Production System, 12. *See also* Lean
      production
  mental models, 24
Toyota Supplier Support Center (TSSC), 14
TPM, 24–25, 39, 53–55
  elimination of losses, 55–56
  Machine Loss Pyramid, 57–58

sample checksheets for, 59–60
  stages of, 61
Training, 52
  standardized work as a basis for, 69
Tree diagrams, 184
Type A pull system, 112
Type B pull system, 112–113
Type C pull system, 113

U

Uneven work, 35. *See also* Mura
Unions, 6
  rights of in Japan, 9–10
United Auto Workers, 6
Unmet needs, 28
Utilization
  law of, 114
  maximization of, 67

V

Value
  definition of, 27–29
  example of, 34–35
Value stream mapping (VSM), 114–118
  business processes and, 118–119
  symbols, 115
Value stream thinking, 118
Vendors, effect of Lean on, 13–14
Visibility, 52–53
Visual management, 34, 39, 41–44, 96, 200
  levels of, 43–44
  office environments, 53
Visual management triangle, 42
Visual systems, 170, 194

W

Waiting, overproduction and, 33
Wakefulness, 193
Wall charts, 42
Warm heart principle, 197
Warning poka-yokes, 132
Warusa-kagen, 58
Waste, 20, 29–30. *See also* Muda
  categories of, 30–34

Wasted motion, 30–31
What-could-be map, 47–48
What-is map, 47–48
Willow Run plant, 5
WIP, 31–32, 90
    control of with pull systems, 95
    defining standards for, 72–73
    pull systems and, 112
Withdrawal kanban, 97–99
Womack, James, 19, 25
Work method deviations, 133
Work piece deviations, 132–133
Work sequence, 72
Work vs. muda, 29–30

Work-in-process. *See* WIP
Workers
    alienation, 6–7
    involvement of, 145 (*See also* Employee
        involvement)
    value of in Lean, 12
Workforce
    characteristics of in craft production, 1
    labor relations in Japan, 10

Z

Zero defects, 124
Zone control, 128–131